Step into Faith

Step into Faith

Mike Mayfield

Editor: Lisa Graybeal

Mike Mayfield Ministries
2019

Copyright © 2019 Michael Mayfield

ISBN: 978-1-7332198-2-2

Cover designer: Mike Mayfield
Editor: Lisa Graybeal

.

For more information, address:
mikemtcmia@gmail.com.

FIRST EDITION

http://www.mikemayfieldministries.org

Introduction

In today's society, people question God's existence. The question arises to whether God is real or not. Then, if God is real, then where is He. God can be seen in every detail of our lives. Our eyes have to open to see Him and our hearts have to be softened. We must spend our time getting to know His ways and His voice. One aspect of God is that He is provider. **Jehovah Jireh** is the name established for God as provider, as stated in Genesis 22:14 (NASB) which says, "And Abraham called the name of that place Jehovah Jireh: as it is said to this day, In the mount of the Lord it shall be seen."

The purpose and intent of this book is to stretch the faith of Christians and help unbelievers believe. The book uses my own life testimony of living off faith for over two years straight. In the two-year period, I did not work a job or receive from the government in the form of food or money. I simply lived off faith. God has stretched my faith and proven He is provider in my life. The book contains powerful testimonies of provision over a 2-year period in my life. I am praying this book stretches believers and opens the eyes and hearts of any unbelievers.

The book is split into two different parts. The first part is a teaching section on faith. The second section is a month to month testimony over the 2-year period of how God provided for me. In the 2-year period, I did not reach out asking for help. I tried to be as hidden as possible going only to God in prayer for all of my needs. I pray God opens your heart, your mind, and the Holy Spirit builds your faith over the course of this book.

Contents

Part 1

Part 2

Acknowledgements

I would like to thank God for getting me through this season and all the friends along the way who empowered, encouraged, and supported me with prayer. Special thanks to Britton Mayfield for his perseverance to push through this tough season. Love you Jesus.

Part 1

Faith

Faith can be defined as having complete trust or confidence in something. Humans utilize faith daily whether they recognize it or not. Every time a person sits down in a chair they put faith in the chair they are sitting in. The motion of sitting down in the chair for it to hold you takes faith. It takes faith believing the chair will hold the person when they sit down in it. If the person does not have faith the chair will hold them, then they will not sit down in it. The simple act of sitting down in a chair for comfort is one example of having faith in something.

Humans also put faith in other people. People utilize putting their faith in other people while they are at the job site. At the job site, it takes having faith in a person to ask them to help you with a task. You have to believe the person will carry out the task you ask them to help you with. If you did not have faith the person could perform the task, then you would not have asked them to help you with the task. Jesus described similar faith in Luke 7 when He meets the centurion.

Luke 7:6-9 (NASB) states "Now Jesus started on His way with them; and when He was not far from the house, the centurion sent friends, saying to Him, 'Lord, do not trouble Yourself further, for I am not worthy to come to You, but just say the word and my servant will be healed. For I also am a man placed under authority, with soldiers under me; and I say to this one, 'Go and he goes, and to another, 'Come! And he comes, and to my slave, 'Do this!' and he does it.'' Now when Jesus heard this, He marveled at him, and turned and said to the crowd that was following Him, 'I say to you, not even in Israel have I found such great faith as this'.

Besides having faith in the natural level, faith can be utilized in the spiritual level. At the elementary level of faith in the spiritual realm, it takes faith to believe that God is real. To obtain salvation, one must believe in their heart Jesus died and rose again. Romans

10:9-10 (NASB) states "that if you confess with your mouth Jesus as Lord and believe in your heart that God raised Him from the dead, you will be saved; for with the heart a person believes, resulting in righteousness, and with the mouth he confesses, resulting in salvation." You must have faith God is real to have any type of spiritual faith which is the foundation of Christianity. Hebrews 11:6 (NASB) states "And without faith it is impossible to please Him, for he who comes to God must believe that He is and that He is a rewarder of those who seek Him."

Once the foundation of faith that God is real and Jesus died for the forgiveness of sins is established in a person's life, then that person can move on to obtaining deeper levels of faith in different areas of God. Romans 8:11 (NASB) states "But if the Spirit of Him who raised Jesus from the dead dwells in you, He who raised Christ Jesus from the dead will also give life to your mortal bodies through His Spirit who dwells in you." After salvation is established, then deeper faith can transpire.

By believing the same Holy Spirit lives in us that lived in Jesus we can live a life like Jesus lived. Acts 10:38 (NASB) states "You know of Jesus of Nazareth, how God anointed Him with the Holy Spirit and with power, and how He went about doing good and healing all who were oppressed by the devil, for God was with Him". A deeper level of faith in God will give you the faith to pray for the sick and they be healed, raise the dead, set people free from demonic influence, and trust God to provide for you because the same spirit that empowered Jesus lives in you. You must have faith to believe all these things are possible through God in which is stated in Mark 10:27 (NASB) by Jesus who said, "With people it is impossible, but not with God; for all things are possible with God".

Before I move forward in the book, I felt led by the Holy Spirit to discuss the gift of faith and God giving various levels of faith. According to the book of Romans, God gives various levels of faith to individuals.

Romans 12:3-8 (NASB) states "For through the grace given to me I say to everyone among you not to think more highly of himself than he ought to think, but to think so as to have sound judgement, as God has allotted to each a measure of faith. For just as we have many members in one body and all the members do not have the same function, so we, who are many, are one body in Christ, and individually members one of another. Since we have gifts that differ according to the grace given to us, each of us is to exercise them accordingly: if prophecy, according to the proportion of his faith; if service, in his serving, or he who teaches, in his teaching, or he who exhorts, in his exhortation; he who gives, with liberality, he who leads with diligence, he who shows mercy, with cheerfulness."

As seen in verse 3, God allots various levels of faith. We can grow in faith by being obedient to the promptings of the Holy Spirit. Luke 16:10 (NASB) states "He who is faithful in a very little thing is faithful also in much, and he who is unrighteous in a very little thing is unrighteous also in much". God knows where you are going, and He will give you the faith you need to utilize as long as you are obedient to the promptings of the Holy Spirit. God gives you the faith you need measured to you, but it can grow as you grow in God if you allow God to stretch it in your life. Abraham grew in his faith. James 2:22 (NASB) states "You see that faith was working, with his works, and as a result of the works, faith was perfected" which proves Abraham's faith was perfected through his obedience.

There is also the gift of faith which is different than possessing faith. 1 Corinthians 12:6-11 (NASB) states "Now there are varieties of gifts, but the same Spirit. And there are varieties of ministries, and the same Lord. There are varieties of effects, but the same God who works all things in all persons. But to each one is given the manifestation of the Spirit for the common good. For to one is given the word of wisdom through the Spirit, and to another the word of knowledge according to the same Spirit, to another faith by the same Spirit, and to another gifts of healing by the one Spirit and to another the effecting of miracles, and to another the prophecy, and to another the distinguishing of spirits, to another various kinds of tongues, and to another the interpretation of tongues. But one and the same Spirit works all these things, distributing to each one individually just as He wills."

The gift of faith mentioned in verse 9 is different than having faith in God. The gift of faith mentioned here is more of a supernatural rising up faith inside of you when it is needed. The gift of faith stirs up and is utilized when needed it is not a constant faith. Gifts are freely given by God according to His grace as stated in Romans 12:6 (NASB) which says "Since we have gifts that differ according to the grace given to us, each of us is to exercise them accordingly: if prophecy, according to the proportion of his faith".

An example of utilizing the gift of faith in my own life to illustrate the gift, occurred one time I was in Wal-Mart shopping. I was walking by a guy who was using a crutch and his knee was bandaged up. When I walked by him, I felt a burden inside of me to pray for him. I exercised the gift of faith in me as I stepped out and prayed for his knee. While praying for his knee, the faith in me was supernatural through the gift of faith to heal his knee. God took all the pain away immediately. Before prayer he could not bend his knee, and after prayer he could bend it fully. He carried the crutch out of Wal-Mart on his shoulder because he did not need it anymore.

Another example of the gift of faith stirring up in me also occurred at Wal-Mart. I walked by a lady who had a bandage on her knee. I felt a strong since of compassion in my heart for her when I walked by her and knew I was supposed to pray for her. I stepped out in faith and asked her if could pray for her. While praying for her, the gift of faith stirred up in me praying for her fractured knee. During prayer, she said she felt her knee tingle and felt a burning like fire go into her knee. God supernaturally gave me the faith that her knee would be healed, and God healed her knee. Now that a foundation of faith is established, I will move on to the topic of trust.

6

Trust

Trust can be defined as having reliability in something. In order to have faith in something, you need to have trust in it. Trust is built over a process of time. For instance, referring to the example of a person sitting down in the chair, it takes having trust the chair will hold you when you sit down in it to have the faith to sit down in the chair. If you did not have trust in the chair to hold you up when you sat down in it, then you would not have the faith to sit down in it to begin with. If the chair broke when you sat down in it, then you are not going to have faith to sit down in the same chair again. Your trust in that chair would be broken because the chair broke when you sat down in it, and you would not trust or have faith in the chair anymore. Instead, you would pick a different chair in which you trust that would hold you up when you sat down in it. Faith and trust go hand in hand together. The same thing applies with the example of working with people on the jobsite. If you do not trust the person you are working with, then you will not have the faith to ask them to do something for you. You will ask another person you have trust in.

On the spiritual level, Christians are called to have trust in God. Once faith is established in a person's life that God is real, then according to teachings by Jesus a Christian is to trust God to provide and take care of them. Two examples from Matthew and Luke show Jesus commanding His disciples not worry about earthly things but to seek God's kingdom and God will provide.

Matthew 6:31-33 (NASB) states "Do not worry then, saying, 'What will we eat?' or 'What will we drink?' or 'What will we wear for clothing?' For the Gentiles eagerly seek all these things; for your heavenly Father knows that you need all these things. But seek first His kingdom and His righteousness, and all these things will be added to you".

Luke 7:22-31(NASB) states "Then Jesus said to his disciples: "Therefore I tell you, do not worry about your life, what you will eat; or about your body, what you will wear. For life is more than food, and the body more than clothes. Consider the ravens: They do not sow or reap, they have no storeroom or barn; yet God feeds them. And how much more valuable you are than birds! Who of you by worrying can add a single hour to your life? Since you cannot do this very little thing, why do you worry about the rest? "Consider how the wild flowers grow. They do not labor or spin. Yet I tell you, not even Solomon in all his splendor was dressed like one of these. If that is how God clothes the grass of the field, which is here today, and tomorrow is thrown into the fire, how much more will he clothe you—you of little faith! And do not set your heart on what you will eat or drink; do not worry about it. For the pagan world runs after all such things, and your Father knows that you need them. But seek his kingdom, and these things will be given to you as well".

These two passages are promises to believers that God will provide for us. All we have to do is have faith and trust Him to do it. The faith part believes, and the trust is the inner knowing and peace we have while waiting on God to do it because you know He is reliable. Trust with God is built more the longer a person walks with God. Hopefully, you are starting to see how faith and trust go hand in hand with each other. The faith part of us believes in God, and the trust part of us is the confidence knowing God is faithful to abide by His word. The bottom line is, faith equals belief in God, and trust equals having confidence that God is reliable. Now, I will move forward to praying, believing, and expectancy in God.

Pray, believe, expect

Once faith and trust in God are established in a Christian's life, they should be developing a daily prayer life with God. To me, prayer is communion with God. Personally, I have a one on one dialogue with God just like I do with a normal person. I talk, and I wait for God to talk back to me. Most of my prayer time consists of me sitting in silence listening to what God has to say to me, or I ask God what is on His heart. Ecclesiastes 5:2 (NASB) states "Do not be hasty in word or impulsive in thought to bring up a matter in the presence of God. For God is in heaven and you are on the earth; therefore, let your words be few."

Jesus taught on prayer saying in Matthew 6:7-8 (NASB)," And when you are praying, do not use meaningless repetition as the Gentiles do, for they suppose that they will be heard for their many words. So, do not be like them; for your Father knows what you need before you ask Him". According to the previous two scriptures, we are not supposed to talk much when we go to God in prayer. If we are not talking much, then that means we are listening to God. The perfect prayer would be praying in the spirit as mentioned in Romans 8:26-27 (NASB) which states "In the same way the Spirit also helps our weakness; for we do not know how to pray as we should, but the Spirit Himself intercedes for *us* with groanings too deep for words; and He who searches the hearts knows what the mind of the Spirit is, because He intercedes for the saints according to *the will of* God".

When we go to God in prayer with the right motive God will answer. 1 John 5:14 (NASB) states "This is the confidence which we have before Him, that, if we ask anything according to His will, He hears us". Also, James 1:2-3 (NASB) states "You lust and do not have; *so,* you commit murder. You are envious and cannot obtain; *so,* you fight and quarrel. You do not have because you do not ask. You ask and do not receive, because you ask with wrong

10

motives, so that you may spend *it* on your pleasures". According to these scriptures, anything we ask according to God's will with the right motive we will receive. What does according to God's will mean? Asking according to God's will simply means asking according to God's promises in the Bible or praying His heart prophetically. For the purposes of this book, I will stick to praying God's promises in the Bible.

Because this book is a testimony of living on the promise of God's provision, I will give an example of praying for His provision in our life. One of God's promises in the Bible is that He will provide for all of our needs which is proven scripture. When it comes to provision, Jesus teaches God already knows what we need before we ask Him.

Matthew 6:31-33 (NASB) states: "So do not worry, saying, 'What shall we eat?' or 'What shall we drink?' or 'What shall we wear?' [32] For the pagans run after all these things, and your heavenly Father knows that you need them. But seek first His kingdom and His righteousness, and all these things will be added to you".

In the previous verses, Jesus is teaching His disciples not to be like the Pharisees seeking the things of the world, but to seek God's Kingdom first and everything will be added to them. God's will for our life is for us to have food and clothing. We are to stand on God's truth in prayer claiming His provision over our lives. All you have to do is simply tell God what you need, then thank Him for already providing it. God already knows what you need before you ask Him. Matthew 6:8 (NASB) states "So do not be like them; for your Father knows what you need before you ask Him". So, simply telling God what you need and thanking Him in advance can be done because provision is a finished work as long as you are seeking God's kingdom and righteousness.

I pulled the thanking God in advance for provision by mimicking the life of Abraham as shown in the book of Romans.

Romans 8:20-21(NASB) states "yet, with respect to the promise of God, he did not waver in unbelief but grew strong in faith, giving glory to God, and being fully assured that what God had promised, He was able also to perform". As the scripture states, Abraham thanked God for the promise in advance before God provided it to him. In the book of Genesis, God promised Abraham a son. Between the time of having the child and God speaking the promise to Abraham, Abraham thanked God for the promise God made to him because he knew God was faithful to fulfil it. Even though Abraham's son had not manifested in the natural yet, Abraham had faith to believe and trust God was good for His word.

Likewise, we have the promise of God providing food and clothing for us according to Jesus' teaching in Matthew 6. Just like Abraham thanked God for his son before he was born, we should thank God for our provision even if we cannot see it in the natural yet. Believing and expecting is manifested in the natural by thanking God for what we need before we ever have it. Instead of letting worry, doubt, and unbelief creep in, simply thank God in advance for providing for your needs. Just have faith in God's word in the Bible and trust while waiting on it to happen knowing God is good for His word as stated in 2 Timothy 2:13 (NASB) which states "If we are faithless, He remains faithful, for He cannot deny Himself".

Expectancy

While writing this book, God prompted me to write a section on expectancy. Webster's defines expectancy as "the act, action, or state of expecting". The Greek word for expectancy is [1]*apokaradokía* which translates to mean the following: properly, thinking forward (literally with head out-stretched), referring to eager, intense expectation. When we pray God's will, or receive a word from God, we must have expectancy it will come to pass in our lives. We are literally supposed to expect God will do what He says He will do or what we ask Him to do when we pray according to His will. We should think forward which means our thought pattern is changed from hoping God will do it to a state of awareness knowing that what we prayed for is going to happen. For example, when you are waiting on your best friend to call you when they said they would call you at 11 A.M. you wait with full expectation they are going to do what they said they will do. While waiting, you anticipate the call expecting it to happen holding the phone in your hand looking at the clock ready at 10:59. The same expectancy you have while anticipating on your best friend to call is the same expectancy you need to have while waiting on God to answer prayer in your life.

We should have excitement while waiting patiently for God to move on His promises in our life. We should be expectant with eager expectation while waiting on God. God is faithful, and He is perfect in all His ways. He provides in ways we would never expect. In the book of Hosea, God provided for the adulteress woman and she was unaware He was providing for her. Hosea 2:5 (NASB) states "For their mother has played the harlot; She who conceived them has acted shamefully. For she said, 'I will go after my lovers, who give me my bread and my water, My wool and my flax, my oil and my drink". This scripture reference is put to here to emphasize even we are unfaithful we can expect God to be faithful. God provides for us at times when we are not even aware it is God doing it. We simply must live in expectation. Living in expectation means we literally know and have peace God will do what He says He is going to do. While waiting, we thank God for His faithfulness by offering Him thanks of praise before we have what we are expecting God to provide because we are expecting God to do what He has promises He will do. After all, "every good thing given and every perfect gift is from above, coming down from the Father of lights, with whom there is no variation or shifting shadow" (James 1:17, NASB).

Words of God

Besides expecting God to provide through prayer, we can also expect God to provide through His word. There are two types of words from God which will be discussed in this section. The first word is the spoken word of God which is also known as the Rhema word. The second word is the Logos word which refers to the inspired word of God also known as the Bible. God led me to put these two words in this section to emphasize you can expect these two kinds of words to come to pass. Jeremiah 1:12 (NASB) states "Then the LORD said to me, "You have seen well, for I am watching over My word to perform it". Also, Isaiah 55:11 (NASB) states "So will My word be which goes forth from My mouth; It will not return to Me empty, without accomplishing what I desire, and without succeeding *in the matter* for which I sent it" (Isaiah 55:11). When God says He will do something with His word, we should be expecting it to happen in our life because it will come to pass in our life.

Rhema word

As stated earlier, the Rhema word is the spoken word of God. The definition for [2]Rhema is "that which is or has been uttered by the living voice, thing spoken word". There are a few diverse ways God has personally given me a Rhema word which came to pass in my life I will use here as an example to help teach you in this section. One-way God gives a Rhema word is when the Holy Spirit highlights a section of scripture while you are reading it. There are times when you read the Bible and literally a few words or one word are highlighted in the Spirit while you are reading it and your eyes are drawn to it. When this happens, the words you read bear witness with your spirit and the word or words literally pop out at your eyes.

One example of this happening in my life to help teach you occurred when I was visiting my family in Tennessee. God told me to go spend a couple days with my son in Tennessee, and I was having trouble dealing with everything happening. I went to the river to meditate on God, and the Holy Spirit told me read the book of James. While reading the book of James, the word "patient" was highlighted every time I came across the word in the first couple of chapters of James. The book of James is a book of wisdom, and the word patient is used more than once in it. God was telling me to be patient through the trial I was going through. I was surrounded with unbelievers and was getting drained with all the ungodliness around me. God highlighted the word to inform me to be patient with the people I was around while going through the trial. As you can see the word "patient" was highlighted and used as a Rhema word to inform me what to do right when I needed it. God also spoke to me "My grace is sufficient" directly to my spirit while highlighting the word "patient" to assure me I could walk through what I was going through with His help at that time.

Another way God uses the Rhema word, which I have also personally experienced in my life, is when He speaks the word to you through someone and it bears witness with your spirit. The word literally comes out of the mouth of another person. God is speaking through the Rhema word through the other person. In my experience, with this type of spoken word God normally confirms His word with two or three people. The scripture reference I have heard to apply to this is 2 Corinthians 13:1 (NASB) which states "This is the third time I am coming to you. Every fact is to be confirmed by the testimony of two or three witnesses". The example which comes to my Spirit to give you here occurred when God spoke to me about what college to attend.

When I was praying for direction on more education, God spoke the word "Liberty" directly to my spirit and I was more than sure God was calling me to Liberty University to take Christian Counseling classes. After God spoke "Liberty" directly to my spirit, I asked God to give me confirmation on it. I knew liberty either meant freedom or to attend college at liberty. Not long after I asked God to confirm Liberty College as His will for my life, He was faithful to fulfill what I asked from Him. A few days after I asked God to give me a confirmation on attending Liberty, while working all I heard throughout the day was the word "Liberty". The word "Liberty" was spoken by numerous people at different job sites where I was a delivery driver at the time. The word "Liberty" was spoken many times by random people numerous days in a row, and each time "Liberty" was said it was bearing witness with my spirit which is how I knew it was God confirming His word. God literally threw it in my face confirming it with numerous people by having them speak the word "Liberty" to me.

Along with God confirming "Liberty" with the Rhema spoken word through people, He used an angel to confirm it as well. I was still uncertain wanting more confirmation before I made the decision and prayed to God again for another confirmation. A day or two after I prayed, I went to the prayer house to pray. While walking to the prayer house, I came across a random girl right beside the prayer house. As I walked by the girl all she said was "I am promoting Liberty today would you like to help" while holding a liberty sign. She was not promoting Liberty College but just liberty as in freedom. I had been going to the prayer house for over 2 years consistently. In over 2 years of going to this place to pray, no one had ever been at that spot promoting anything. I told her no, but I did pray for her to receive help from God. I left the spot and came back not even two minutes later to ask her a question and she was gone. Hebrews 13:2 (NASB) states "Do not neglect to show hospitality to strangers, for by this some have entertained angels without knowing it". Don't box God He will speak to you if you are available and listening even if it's with an angel. After all, angels are messengers from God. Hebrews 1:14 (NASB) states "Are they not all ministering spirits, sent out to render service for the sake of those who will inherit salvation?".

Logos

Now I will briefly discuss the logos word of God. The Greek translation of [3]logos simply means the following: "word, speech, principle, or thought". For the purposes of the teaching in this book, I felt led to just use the translation which means word. I feel like God is leading me to just teach on standing on the word or the Bible in this book. The Bible is full of promises. There are way too many promises in the Bible to list in this chapter. I encourage you to study them and look them up on your own. To give proof the Bible is full of promises I felt led to put the scripture Ephesians 6:1-3 (NASB) states "Children, obey your parents in the Lord, for this is right. Honor your father and mother (which is the first commandment with a promise), so that it may be well with you, and that you may live long on the earth." Like I said, besides this scripture there are many other scriptures in the Bible with promises. I encourage you to ask God to help you seek them out and make time to do it, so you will know what promises and truths to stand on.

Standing on the Word of God

For the purposes of this book, I am going to teach you how to stand on the logos word of God. I felt strongly by the Holy Spirit to put this section in here. As Christians, it is easy to get caught up in doubt, unbelief, and questioning God especially when life circumstances get tough. Instead of expecting God to do something in our lives, we focus on the circumstances of our lives and our faith waivers. The promises listed in the Bible, which were briefly mentioned in the previous chapter, are what we are called to stand on even when all life circumstances say otherwise. 2 Corinthians 5:7 (NASB) states "for we walk by faith, not by sight God".

God has brought me to a deep personal revelation of His provision in my life. I am the point I know for a fact God will always provide for me. I no longer question His provision in my life. I have an expectancy mindset when it comes to God's provision in my life almost to the point I rarely even pray for provision any more. Provision is one of God's promises in the Bible. If I am out of food, I go to a scripture which states God will provide my food and I declare it over my life thanking God for it even before it has manifested in my life. I have an expectancy knowing God is going to bring me food after I pray for it. I call this standing on the logos word of God. All the promises in the Bible can be done like this. It is just a matter of having expectancy and patience because we do not always know God's timing on it and when it will manifest in the natural. We just know God will do it unless told otherwise by Him.

Since this book is mostly about living on faith while emphasizing and focusing on God's provision in our lives, I feel led by the Holy Spirit to quote Isaiah 51 here. I remember numerous times during this over 2-year journey of living off faith I had no idea how I was going to make it in the natural. While questioning how I was going to survive, God led me to Isaiah 51 numerous times. Isaiah 51:1-3 (NASB) states "Listen to me, you who pursue righteousness,

Who seek the LORD: Look to the rock from which you were hewn and to the quarry from which you were dug. "Look to Abraham your father And to Sarah who gave birth to you in pain; When *he was but* one I called him, Then I blessed him and multiplied him. "Indeed, the LORD will comfort Zion; He will comfort all her waste places. And her wilderness He will make like Eden, And her desert like the garden of the LORD; Joy and gladness will be found in her, Thanksgiving and sound of a melody".

God took me to Isaiah 51 numerous times during this journey of living on faith. I meditated particularly on the verse which says, "And her wilderness He will make like Eden." While meditating on this verse, I imagined what the Garden of Eden was like before the fall of man and the curse. There was no thistles or thorns I honestly cannot imagine to the full extent of what the garden was like. The point is God gave me the promise He would make the wilderness I was in like the Garden of Eden when I needed provision in my life.

The promise God spoke through Isaiah 51 is amazing and all I had to do was stand on it. I stood on it by thanking God for what He was going to do in my life before I could ever see it in the natural. I simply thanked God for doing what He promised me He would do without seeing yet in the natural. In my morning devotion when God led me to the scripture each time I needed provision, I simply thanked God for making my wilderness like Eden. Every single time God gave me this scripture in the morning, God provided for me the same day. He stood faithful to His logos word and made my wilderness like Eden. I simply quoted and declared the scripture over myself and thanked Him for doing what He said He would do even before I saw it manifest in the natural.

Going back to the scripture in Matthew 6:8 (NASB) which states "So do not be like them; for your Father knows what you need before you ask Him". And Psalm 139:4 (NASB) states "Even before there is a word on my tongue, Behold, O LORD, You know it all". God already knows what we need before we ask Him and knows our words we speak before we speak them. Standing on these truths in Bible means we can ask and thank God in advance before we see a manifestation of what we are asking for in the natural. Proverbs 10:3 (NASB) states "The LORD will not allow the righteous to hunger, But He will reject the craving of the wicked". God is a good Father and is not going to let you go hungry if you are doing and seeking His will in your life.

The key is to stand on and declare the truth of the Bible over ourselves and not let doubt and unbelief creep in. When we declare the word over ourselves, which means literally speaking the verse of the Bible out loud over ourselves, we are standing on the truth. Jesus confirms God's word as truth in John 17:17 (NASB) which states "Sanctify them in the truth; Your word is truth". The building of faith takes time. Romans 10:17 (NASB) states "faith comes by hearing and hearing by the word of God". Faith can be built by declaring it because when we hear it faith builds in us. After verbally declaring the promises in the Bible over your life with your mouth, next you should thank God for making them happen even though they have not manifested yet

Another example of me standing on a promise in the Bible, is when God healed me of Hepatitis C. Before I was saved, I contracted Hepatitis C from sharing needles with other people who had the virus. At the time I contracted the disease, it was still incurable. I was learning the Bible well attending Teen Challenge ministry and knew the Bible said that God heals all our diseases. I was familiar with the verses on healing in Isaiah 53, and in 1 Peter 2:24 (NASB) which states by Jesus stripes we were healed which is paraphrased. Psalm 103:3 states "Who pardons all your iniquities, Who heals all your diseases." I knew God's truth in the Word that God healed because of Jesus's sacrifice on the cross and knew Hepatitis C was a disease.

I stood on the truth of God's word which states He heals all our diseases. One night I went to a miracle service and got prayer. The lady had been used by God to heal incurable diseases and I knew

God was going to heal me. Standing on the truth of the word and having faith God would use the lady to heal me, I went forward for prayer at the altar call. Her prayer laid me out on the ground, and I knew God healed me. For over a year after receiving prayer from her, I stood on the truth that God healed me spoke God healed me and thanked God for healing me even though I had no clue in the natural other than relying on faith if I was physically healed. It was literally over a year before I returned to the doctor to be checked for the disease. I stood on faith and declared by faith I was healed. If anyone asked me about having Hepatitis C I told them I had it, but God healed me. I found out close to a year later I was healed miraculously in the natural. The doctors literally had no explanation because the disease was still in my body, but it was dead. The doctor told me "I was a very lucky man" and I responded "No, God is good". The emphasis being I stood on the truth of the word and thanked God for the healing after the lady of God prayed for me.

Standing on the spoken Word

Standing on the Rhema word, also known as the spoken word of God, is done the same way as standing on the logos or written word of God. Whatever promise God has spoken to you, either directly to your spirit or through someone else, you declare it over yourself the same way you declare the scripture promises over yourself. You war over the promise in the spirit thanking God for what was spoken until it manifests in the natural. We do not know God's timing on the promise or if it will even come to pass while we are alive, but we stand on faith trusting God is good for His word. For example, Hebrews 11:38-39 (NASB) states "And all these, having gained approval through their faith, did not receive ⌊was promised, because God had provided something better for us, so that apart from us they would not be made perfect." God is faithful to keep his word, but we have to walk by faith trusting God will bring the promise He has spoken in our life to pass. We build faith by declaring the promise and thanking God for it until it manifests in the natural.

An example of this in my own life to give you an example occurred when God promised to pour out provision into my life to visit my son. The word God spoke to my spirit was this: "This weekend is My gift to you. I've seen your tears. I've heard you hearts cry to be with your son. I'm going to pour out My provision in your life. Don't worry about money. There are people there who need you. You are a bright light child. My spirit is strong within you. You have authority exercise it. Don't be afraid of what might happen expect good things to happen."

When God gave me this was I was living in Charlotte, North Carolina which was close to a 7 hour drive for my son. The days leading up to the visit God had me giving my money away to homeless people. God had me handing out twenty-dollar bills to random homeless people as led by the Spirit. When I got the word to go see my son, I literally had $20 in the bank account and the gas light was on in the truck. In the back of my mind I was honestly doubting God. I was not walking by faith and not by sight I was more walking by sight and not by faith. The morning I was going to drive to Tennessee I received a text message from a mentor to come pick up money from his workplace. The text message came literally an hour before I was going to leave. The mentor said God put it on his heart to give me money and it was close to $80 and bought the gas I needed to get to Tennessee.

After I got to Tennessee, God provided every one of my meals for me. The only time I had to pay for my food was on the drive to and on the drive back from Tennessee. The entire time I was in Tennessee people took me out to eat and paid for my food. God provided all my meals for me. While in Tennessee visiting my son, God put it on other people's heart to give me more money and gas. I literally accumulated close to $300 over the course of two days along with all my meals provided. God told me He was going to pour out His hand of provision in my life to provide for the trip and not to worry about money. He was faithful to keep His spoken promise to my spirit. I simply stepped out in faith when God led me. Seeing God's provision on the trip after having the word spoken to me built my faith on His spoken rhema word to my spirit. Prior to this, I somewhat questioned His speaking to my spirit.

Once again Matthew 6:33 (NASB) states "Seek you first His kingdom and righteousness and all these things will be added unto you." While on the trip to Tennessee I kept God first and was used to heal, encourage, and build others up. God used me to speak life into a gas station clerk by a word of knowledge about his personal life. While at a rest stop on the way to Tennessee God healed a guy who had imbalance in vision while driving. God healed him instantly. At a restaurant, God gave me numerous words of knowledge about our waitress to the point she blushed along with encouraging words from God. God healed my son of a headache as he was going to bed. He stated he had a headache and I prayed for him and God healed him instantly. My son looked at me and said "thank you daddy" and I pointed him back to God for the healing. God also healed my mom of back pain after I felt her pain in my back with a word of knowledge. Also, I gave money to others while on the trip as led by the Spirit. My heart's sole ambition was to seek God's Kingdom first.

Hearing from God

Now, I will discuss a few different ways you can hear from God. Because the subject of this book is about living on faith, an extensive teaching on hearing from God will not be detailed. There are many other excellent books on hearing from God out there. I pray for God to lead you to the right one if you are wanting more information on hearing God's voice. The few ways on hearing God's voice I will very briefly describe in this book include: God speaking directly to your heart, God speaking to you through people, God speaking to you through the Bible, and God using dreams and visions to speak to you.

The first way of hearing from God that will be discussed is by God speaking directly to our hearts. Almost every single time God has had me step out in faith in giving, God has spoken the word directly to my heart. When God speaks to my heart, it is simply words put in my heart or with a burden. The voice sounds like my own voice except it comes straight to my heart. If what is on my heart does not go away or I start to get convicted for being disobedient to the Holy Spirit, then I know for a fact it is God speaking to my heart. The tug to do the action from the Holy Spirit sticks in my heart. The unction is inside my body in my heart, so I do not doubt that it is God using the Holy Spirit. The amount of money to give and the words which normally go something like "give him $10" are imprinted into my heart. The words are literally imprinted by God through the Holy Spirit on the inside of my heart. There is no mistaking it is God speaking to my heart. As stated earlier, the feeling inside of my heart normally does not go away until either I am obedient, or I get convicted for being disobedient. It is literally having an inner voice inside your heart. The words are put there by the Holy Spirit.

Sometimes the unction to give money away is so strong it literally burdens my heart. When the burden comes, there is no mistaking it is God. The burden is carrying God's heart for the person. The burden is deep in my heart and hurts sometimes. The burden from God can be described as an extremely heavy unction inside of the heart. There is no mistaking when you are getting a burden from God. The feeling is incomparable, and you cannot mistake it is God doing it inside of you because it is not a natural occurrence. The burden is a supernatural experience. It literally feels like my spiritual heart is shriveling together inside me and it causes me to bend over in my physical body. The pain from the burden comes a little below the center of my chest down towards my stomach inside of my body. The burden comes with a specific amount of money to give to the specific person. The burden normally starts when I drive or walk by someone God wants me to minister to. The burden won't go away until either I do what God says or pray it out.

The second way I will discuss of hearing from God comes through God speaking to you using people. God will use people to speak His word through their mouths. Every time God has spoken to me this way, He has used two or three different people to say the same thing within a short amount of time. Normally when God speaks this way two people say the same thing the same day. A person can tell if it is God or not because it normally comes as scripture or a phrase and it bears witness with your spirit. For example, God told me to give a testimony to a guy walking and he responded to me "With God all things are possible". Later the same day I got a text message saying, "With God all things are possible". Another example occurred when a pastor told me to "be thankful for the little things". Later the same day, I got a text message from a friend saying, "be thankful in the little things". These are just two examples of numerous times God has used people to speak to me. God will make it clear to you what He wants you to do so do not worry about it. You will know it is God speaking when it happens just listen and be obedient when you hear His voice.

The final way I will discuss hearing from God is when God uses dreams and visions to speak to you. When you have a God dream, you will know because the dream will be vivid with symbolism that is distinct, and God will sometimes speak to you in the dream as well. Sometimes He even uses scriptures and angels in the dream to speak to you as well. One example of God using a dream to correct me occurred when I was losing focus on God. The dream God gave me to correct me was a dream about love, serving, and humility.

The dream consisted of me sitting in a big class room under a prophetic mentor I sit under in real life. In the dream, before I went to sit in the big classroom with tables and chairs was I talking to my prophetic mentor while fixing a drink. I only fixed the drink for myself and did not think to offer the prophetic mentor or anyone else a drink. In the dream, the lack of servitude on my behalf was highlighted into focus. Next, I went into the classroom and sat down while my prophetic mentor was teaching. While in the classroom, I did not listen to what the prophetic mentor was teaching. The mentor asked me a question in the dream, and I missed it. In the dream, I could tell I was being haughty like I knew more than anyone else in the class. I was being prideful as if I was above every other person in the room. Pride is something I struggle with sometimes. In the dream, when I missed the question my friend laughed at me and I actually spoke the word "humility" in the dream. After I left the classroom in the dream, I went to take a shower. While running water in the shower I took an extremely, extremely, extremely long time to find clothes to wear. I knew God was emphasizing the delay in time to inform me I needed patience for the task at hand. God used this dream to show me I needed to start serving again, be humbler, listen more, and be patient. There was more symbolism in the dream, and I am sure God was speaking more than just these main points, but I know for a fact God was using the dream to correct me in these areas of my life because I was slipping in these areas.

Another example of hearing from God in a dream is when God told me I was going to receive an impartation which occurred at the beginning of 2017. I was doing a fast to start the year off and one night during this fast God gave me a dream of going to the airport. While in the airport waiting on luggage, a prophet mentor I sit under in real life just arrived at the airport terminal from getting off the plane from a flight. He was with his friend who I personally know in real life. They both came up to me in the dream and spoke to me. Next in the dream, the prophet mentor laid hands on me and started praying saying "You are going to receive an impartation of joy". In the dream, they were laying hands on me praying and I fell out in the spirit. The impartation was powerful in the dream. The dream ended shortly after that and it was not long after the dream occurred, I started having more joy in real life.

Faith in action

At this part in the book, I will switch back to what faith looks like in the current culture. Today, we have so many forms of provision it can be easy to not place trust in God for are needs and go to other sources. We have government help with food supplements, credit cards, loans, people to help us by asking, and other such methods to place faith and trust in other than God. But what would happen if we put our full trust in God to provide for our every need like He says to do in His word? Does God still provide in the modern society? To answer these questions, I am going to use testimonies in my own life where for a period of over 2 years I did not work or ask from help for anyone including the government, family members, or friends. When I needed something, I simply prayed for it. Remarkably, God proved Himself faithful to His word.

If we have faith and trust in God knowing He will provide for all our needs, then how do we walk it out in life? James 2:26 (NASB) states "For as the body without the spirit is dead, so faith without works is dead also". We are supposed to walk out our faith in God by doing works along with believing in God. James 2 also gives the example of Abraham sacrificing his son Isaac. James 2:21-23 (NASB) states "Was not Abraham our father justified by works when he offered Isaac his son on the altar? Do you see that faith was working together with his works, and by works faith was made perfect? And the Scripture was fulfilled which says, "Abraham believed God, and it was accounted to him for righteousness." And he was called the friend of God." Abraham proved he had faith in God with his works to sacrifice his son Isaac. We should follow Abraham's example in our own lives as Christians. After all, we are called "to walk by faith and not by sight" as stated in 2 Corinthians 5:7 (NASB).

Besides having faith God is real, we should have acts of faith working in our lives. The acts of faith should come through the promptings of the Holy Spirit. Almost every time God has had me give to a person, pray for a person, or give a prophetic word to a person I have felt the prompting by the Holy Spirit in my heart. Sometimes the prompting is faint and sometimes it is a heavy burden. Either way, the prompting from God through the Holy Spirit in me has been there. Exercising our faith requires us to follow through on the promptings God gives us regardless if it makes sense in the natural. Honestly, many times God has had me step out in faith and it has not made sense in the natural. Each time we are obedient to the promptings of the Holy Spirit we are exercising faith.

One example of God having me step out in faith following the promptings of the Holy Spirit is when praying for the sick. One time I was driving, and God gave me a heavy burden for a lady waiting at a bus stop as I drove by her. I pulled my truck over and went to the lady telling her God told me to stop and pray for her. When I walked up to her, I felt pain in my back and I knew God was giving me a word of knowledge that she had back pain. I asked her if she had back pain and she replied yes. I gave her testimonies of how God has taken all the pain in other people through prayer. She let me pray for her and God instantly took away all her back pain. Being obedient to the prompting of the Holy Spirit to stop and talk the lady while driving by her and then following the Holy Spirit's prompting to pray for back pain I exercised faith. It took faith with works to stop and talk to the lady while driving and ask her if she had back pain. This is one example of what faith with works looks like. For the purpose of this book, faith in giving and receiving will be discussed more than giving prophetic words or promptings to pray for people.

God as provider

Earlier in the book, I established the foundation of God being provider. God clearly states we are not to worry about the things of this world, but we are to seek His kingdom first and He will provide for all of our needs in Matthew 6. It is easy to say God is provider when you have a job and a regular paycheck coming in or are fully established with money in the bank. With a guaranteed paycheck or having money to spend in the bank, it is easy to say God is provider. But can you say and truly mean that God is provider when you have no source of income and food? Will you still have the faith and trust in God to provide for all of your needs without a source of income? God promises us He will provide for us if we seek His kingdom first as stated in Matthew 6:33 (NASB) "Seek you first His Kingdom and righteousness and all these things will be added to you".

Using examples in my life of living on faith, I will prove God is provider without working a job or asking anyone for help to build faith in others. Each time I needed provision in my life during this time period, I followed Abraham's example discussed earlier in this book of standing on God's promise and thanking God in advance for providing even when it was not there yet in the natural. I will also use me stepping out in faith in giving when prompted by the Holy Spirit to give to others. God used the process of giving to others while standing on faith to stretch me. God had me give my last amount of money or food on faith to others, and I simply stood on faith thanking God in advance for His provision in my life after giving what I had away even when it was not there yet in the natural because God promises us He will provide for us if we are seeking His kingdom and righteousness and I was seeking His Kingdom and righteousness.

God's kingdom works different than the world's standard. God has principles established in giving. Luke 6:38 (NASB) states "Give, and it will be given to you. They will pour into your lap a good measure—pressed down, shaken together, *and* running over. For by your standard of measure it will be measured to you in return". Once again God promises what we give out we will receive. Galatians 6:7 (NASB) states "Do not be deceived, God is not mocked; for whatever a man sows, this he will also reap". To go along with that, we reap what we sow. 2 Corinthians 9:6-11 (NASB) "Now this *I say*, he who sows sparingly will also reap sparingly, and he who sows bountifully will also reap bountifully. Each one *must do* just as he has purposed in his heart, not grudgingly or under compulsion, for God loves a cheerful giver. And God is able to make all grace abound to you, so that always having all sufficiency in everything, you may have an abundance for every good deed; as it is written, "He scattered abroad, he gave to the poor, his righteousness endures forever." Now He who supplies seed to the sower and bread for food will supply and multiply your seed for sowing and increase the harvest of your righteousness; you will be enriched in everything for all liberality, which through us is producing thanksgiving to God".

According to previous scriptures whatever we give to others we will receive. God uses the principle of sowing and reaping. When you give something away when prompted by God, you will receive the same thing back in return. For example, if you need love then you give out love to others. If you need encouragement, then you give out encouragement to others. The same principle works in giving money. If you give money away, then you will reap money. You probably know the principle of tithing. God states in Malachi 3:8-10 (NASB) states ""Will a man rob God? Yet you are robbing Me! But you say, 'How have we robbed You?' In tithes and offerings. You are cursed with a curse, for you are robbing Me, the whole nation *of you*! Bring the whole tithe into the storehouse, so that there may be food in My house, and test Me now in this," says the LORD of hosts, "if I will not open for you the windows of heaven and pour out for you a blessing until it overflows". The standard minimum we are to give is our first fruits, but I am referring to giving beyond tithing in sowing and reaping.

For the purposes of this book, I will be discussing giving beyond tithing. God has molded me to give by being led by the Holy Spirit and living off faith. I pay tithes, but I also try to give any other time I am prompted by God through the Holy Spirit. Each time I have given away to others, God has been faithful to provide for me. The timing is not always right when you give away to others you immediately receive back. I honestly do not know how God times it but His timing is perfect as stated in Psalm 18:30 (NASB) which says "As for God, His way is blameless; The word of the LORD is tried; He is a shield to all who take refuge in Him". I do know there have been times God has had me give my last amount of food or money on faith to receive what I needed not long after stepping out in faith in giving. I know that God is faithful despite human imperfections of doubt or unbelief as stated in 2 Timothy 2:13(NASB) which states "If we are faithless, He remains faithful, for He cannot deny Himself".

Part 2

Faith in action

Now that some basic foundations have in faith, trust, God's provision, praying, and hearing from God has been established, I can discuss what faith looks like in action. To start this chapter Hebrews 11 will be quoted because it is known as the faith chapter.

Hebrews 11 (NASB)

"Now faith is the assurance of *things* hoped for, the conviction of things not seen. For by it the men of old gained approval. By faith we understand that the worlds were prepared by the word of God, so that what is seen was not made out of things which are visible. By faith Abel offered to God a better sacrifice than Cain, through which he obtained the testimony that he was righteous, God testifying about his gifts, and through faith, though he is dead, he still speaks. By faith Enoch was taken up so that he would not see death; and he was not found because God took him up; for he obtained the witness that before his being taken up he was pleasing to God. And without faith it is impossible to please *Him*, for he who comes to God must believe that He is and *that* He is a rewarder of those who seek Him. By faith Noah, being warned *by God* about things not yet seen, in reverence prepared an ark for the salvation of his household, by which he condemned the world, and became an heir of the righteousness which is according to faith. By faith Abraham, when he was called, obeyed by going out to a place which he was to receive for an inheritance; and he went out, not knowing where he was going. By faith he lived as an alien in the land of promise, as in a foreign *land*, dwelling in tents with Isaac and Jacob, fellow heirs of the same promise; for he was looking for the city which has foundations, whose architect and builder is God. By faith even Sarah herself received ability to conceive, even beyond the proper time of life, since she considered Him faithful who had promised. Therefore, there was born even of one man, and him as good as dead at that, *as many descendants* as the stars of heaven in number, and innumerable as the sand which by the seashore. All these died in faith, without receiving the promises, but having seen them and having welcomed them from a distance and having confessed that they were strangers and exiles on the earth. For those who say such things make it clear that they are seeking a country of their own. And indeed, if they had been thinking of that *country* from which they went out, they would have had opportunity to return. But as it is, they desire a better *country*, that is, a heavenly one. Therefore, God is not ashamed to be called their God; for He has prepared a city for them. By faith Abraham, when he was tested, offered up Isaac, and he who had received the promises was offering up his only begotten *son*; *it was he* to whom it was said, "In Isaac your descendants shall be called." He considered that God is able to raise *people* even from the dead, from which he also received him back as a type. By faith Isaac blessed Jacob and Esau, even regarding things to come. By faith Jacob, as he was dying, blessed each of the sons of Joseph, and worshiped, *leaning* on the top of his staff. By faith Joseph, when he was dying, made mention of the exodus of the sons of Israel, and gave orders concerning his bones. By faith Moses, when he was born, was hidden for three months by his parents, because they saw he was a beautiful child; and they were not afraid of the king's edict. By faith Moses, when he had grown up, refused to be called the son of Pharaoh's daughter, choosing rather to endure ill-treatment with the people of God than to enjoy the passing pleasures of sin, considering the reproach of Christ greater riches than the treasures of Egypt; for he was looking to the reward. By faith he left Egypt, not fearing the wrath of the king; for he endured, as seeing Him who is unseen. By faith he kept the Passover and the sprinkling of the blood, so that he who destroyed the firstborn would not touch them. By faith they passed through the Red Sea as though *they were passing* through dry land; and the Egyptians, when they attempted it, were drowned. By faith the walls of Jericho fell down after they had been encircled for seven days. By faith Rahab the harlot did not perish along with those who were disobedient, after she had welcomed the spies in peace and what more shall I say? For time will fail me if I tell of Gideon, Barak, Samson, Jephthah, of David and Samuel and the prophets, who by faith conquered kingdoms, performed *acts of* righteousness, obtained promises, shut the mouths of lions, quenched the power of fire, escaped the edge of the sword, from weakness were made strong, became mighty in war, put foreign armies to flight. Women received *back* their dead by resurrection; and others were tortured, not accepting their release, so that they might obtain a better resurrection; and others experienced mockings and scourgings, yes, also chains and imprisonment. They were stoned, they were sawn in two, they were tempted, they were put to death with the sword; they went about in sheepskins, in goatskins, being destitute, afflicted, ill-treated (*men* of whom the world was not worthy), wandering in deserts and mountains and caves and holes in the ground. And all these, having gained approval through their faith, did not receive what was promised, because God had provided something better for us, so that apart from us they would not be made perfect."

One can build by faith listening to the word of God and testimonies. Romans 12:17 (NASB) states "So faith *comes* from hearing, and hearing by the word of Christ." Because the purpose of this book is to build faith, personal testimonies of God's provision will be listed in excess to boost your faith.

In the beginning: Building blocks of faith: Missouri

This whole journey of me living on faith started after I graduated from Teen Challenge ministry and stopped working for their ministry full time. I was living in Missouri and living on faith. I had no job because I have a criminal record which prevented me from obtaining most jobs and God shut certain doors purposefully. At this point, I was getting food stamps from the government, but I had no other help. God put a pastor in my life who was well founded in living on faith and used the statement "your blessings come from blessing other people" on a regular basis. Basically, he was well founded in sowing and reaping. I had learned God's voice by this time in my life by spending a lot of time with God at Teen Challenge and working in the ministry along with being discipled by men who were led by the Holy Spirit. I had accustomed myself to listening to God's voice and being led by the Holy Spirit.

At this time, I was helping out in a few different ministries in Missouri. I stayed in Missouri for a six-month period. I did not work at all outside of ministries while in Missouri. I applied for over 300 jobs in the area within a matter of six months to have no job offer or interview offer until I was leaving Missouri which is how I knew God had his hand on shutting the door to work. One time I ran out of food stamps before the renewal date and I had no way to get more. I prayed to God for help with food. I had no relatives in Missouri and my family could not help me with food money. God provided rent money during this time through my family; they paid the rent the entire time I was in Missouri. I see it as God providing. The time I ran out of food stamps and had no money to get food I simply prayed to God telling Him I needed food. After praying for food, I called the food stamp card to check my balance and my account had been accredited an extra close to $50 a month. I never called the office and never asked for an increase. When I filled out the papers, I was told I could not get an increase because I was single living by myself. God answered my prayer by supernaturally giving me an increase to my monthly food stamp total.

Another time while living in Missouri, I was completely out of money and needed money to wash my clothes. I did not have my own washer and dryer, so I had to pay to do my laundry. Once again, I prayed to God telling him I needed money to wash clothes. After praying, I started thanking God for His provision in my life even though I did not see it yet. I felt a strong unction from the Holy Spirit to take a walk after I prayed. During this time, I lived within one mile of Mississippi River and I would go watch barges go up and down it while praying there. I left my apartment out of obedience to the prompting of the Holy Spirit and walked down to the Mississippi River. Once I arrived at the river, a regular boat was at the river gas station. I felt heavy in my spirit to ask the people if they needed help because they looked kind of stranded. They asked if I could take them to the gas station to get gas and I agreed. I drove them to the gas station and they gave me $20 without me asking them for money. God provided money to wash my clothes by them paying me for helping them. All I did was listen to the promptings from the Holy Spirit to walk to the river and to help the people on the boat. The prayer to have money to wash my clothes got answered.

To stretch your faith a little further in the supernatural another night once again I had no money. I remember it as if it just happened. It was a Saturday night and I was not going to be able to make it to church the next day because I did not have enough gas to drive to church and I had no money. I got on my hands and knees and I prayed to God telling Him I needed gas money to get to church. I needed a miracle. I went to bed not knowing how I was going to get to church the next day. At about 3 A.M I woke up and looked out the window of my apartment randomly and my car was missing. I immediately panicked and called the cops to tell them my car was missing. The cops told me they would come to my house.

While I was waiting on the cops to arrive at my apartment, my car pulled up outside my apartment. I immediately went outside to my car. Once I got outside, the driver who stole the car got out of it. We both kind of stared at each with 'deer in headlights' look. The driver who got out of the car then said, "I put gas in it for you" and then took off running. I yelled some un-Christlike obscenity as he sped away on foot. Then I went and looked in my car and realized the driver used my spare key. Once I was in the car, I felt the electricity and energy from God's presence stronger than I had ever felt before in my car. The anointing in the car was so strong the hairs stood on my body stood straight up from the electricity. I then realized God had sent an angel to put gas in my car. At that point, I repented for yelling the obscenity. Not long after the angel left, the cops arrived, and I explained everything that happened to them and they thought I was crazy. To this day I still have no idea how the angel got my spare key which was in my wallet. God knows. God answered the prayer for gas and I made it to church the next morning.

There were a few times while living in Missouri God had me give my last dollar or few dollars for church offerings. Almost every time God had me step out in faith giving the last of my money, the next day or two I would get a call from my family telling me they were sending me money. Numerous times I gave my last $5 or $10 to the ministry not knowing how I was going to make it to get $50 to $100 deposited in the bank within the next few days. The season in Missouri was coming to an end. I felt God was calling me to Bible College in Concord, North Carolina. God confirmed the calling when I got accepted to the college then someone gave me $2000 in cash to go. I prayed to God if it was His will for me to go to the college for Him to provide for me. I never asked for the money the person simply handed it to me. I knew when they handed me the money God was providing for me to move to Concord, North Carolina.

Take me deeper God: Stretching in Bible College

Once I got to Concord, North Carolina I thought I already had a lot of faith in God and I wanted more. My heart burned and desired for God and I wanted to go deeper in Him. I prayed for the Lord to take me deeper on several occasions. Praying God take me deeper is a dangerous prayer because in order to go deeper you must be stretched. The stretching process is not a fun process. Upon entering Bible College, I had a job. God provided a job on the first day I arrived which was another prayer request answered. I said to God if it was His will for me to go to Charlotte for Him to provide a job for me right when I got there. After working a few weeks at the job, I was getting persecuted on the jobsite for being a Christian. A co-worker set me up asking my viewpoint on lesbians and gays with a gay co-worker working beside me. I did not know the coworker was gay. I gave the Christian answer to the person who asked me the question, and the gay coworker started crying. Next, they told management and other co-workers what I said about what happens if a gay person does not repent. I got in trouble with management, and co-workers started being rude to me taking the gay co-workers side. I ended up quitting the job due to the persecution. After quitting, I had no idea how I was going to pay my bills.

The prayer for God to take me deeper was getting answered in a way I was not expecting it. At first, I was worried because my faith and trust was in my job and not in God to provide. I started praying to God for Him to help me with money. Leadership was aware of what was going on because I reported the persecution to them, and they responded God is provider while giving testimonies of God's provision in the lives of other people. During this time, God started stretching my faith in provision. I was getting food stamps, so I did not have to worry about food. My faith for God to provide food with prayer was not established yet. The first time I needed to pay my phone bill after losing the job I prayed. My phone was about to get disconnected and I had no way of paying for the bill. The Holy Spirit reminded me how God provided for me while living in Missouri. I never told anyone I needed financial help besides telling people I quit the job. After praying, a friend picked me up and drove me to church. Once we go to the church, he handed me $50. He told me "God told me to give you this". I realized it was God providing for my phone bill because it was almost exactly the amount I needed to pay the bill.

One night at a church meeting it was heavy in my heart to tell the group I was struggling with money. I had prayed and prayed for God to provide while getting behind in almost all of my bills. I was a month behind on rent and utility bills. I never asked anyone for financial help. I confessed to the group I needed prayer and explained what was going on to them. They started praying for me and when they were through praying a lady was prompted by the Holy Spirit to speak. She said, "We are supposed to help Mike there is a strong unction in my spirit to help him". Being led by the Holy Spirit, the group gave me close to a $1000. After tithing, I paid all my bills off and had gas money. A few a weeks later, I was out of both gas and money and never told anyone. At the end of a men's prayer meeting, I was handed close to $50 by the men. I never asked or told anyone I needed help. I prayed to God earlier that morning asking Him to help me with money. They simply said, "God knows what you need" while handing me the money. Once again God provided for my needs.

I was actively looking for jobs during this time. I was going to job interviews when I had them, but God kept the door shut. One time I was driving, and I had no money and was almost out of gas. I was crying out to God and thanking Him for provision having no clue how I was going to make it in the natural. I was literally driving down the road while almost out of gas and had no money. After crying out to God, the telephone rang. It was the church I attended at the time and they said I needed to come pick up an envelope that an anonymous person had donated money to me. I never told a single person I needed help I simply cried out to God while driving down the road. God used a person to once again provide gas money for me.

I was in Bible College and unemployed for close to 3 months at this point. After the group meeting, I still had to pay rent two more times. I never told anyone I needed help. Each time I needed the money for rent and utilities, I prayed to God and thanked Him for His provision. Each concurrent month I needed the money, a random person handed me an envelope with $500. He simply said, "God knows what you need, and God bless you" each time he handed me an envelope. Once again God provide for my needs and I never told a person I needed the help. Not long after receiving the envelopes with money, I got a job and was able to provide for myself. At the end of the semester at Bible College I was looking for a new place to stay and praying for God's direction. I did not have enough money saved up to get my own place and had no prospects for roommates. Someone randomly came up to me one day and told me you can stay at this house in my room. I am moving out and I paid your rent for you for the summer. God provided for me a place to stay for the summer and I never asked anyone. I simply prayed, believed, and expected God provide.

The stretching continues

After finishing the semester off at Bible College, I took a break from full time school. Instead of going to school, I worked a job and took part-time classes. I got a new job which came with an increase in pay. Once my income increased the stretching increased. God started stretching me in giving. During this time, I was still actively involved in helping ministries and attending ministry functions. I did not attend Bible college full time though. While helping at different ministry functions and street witnessing, God had me give to others to stretch my faith.

The first area of giving God stretched me in was committing to give to missionaries. God literally had me giving close to $200 a month to missionaries. During this time, I was working on minimum wage plus tip money averaging about 35 hours of work per week. My total pay a week was never over $400. As you can see, I did not have a lot of income to give away. I simply had to trust God to provide when I gave money away. During this time, God once again put it on someone's heart to give me a place to stay for free and I did not have pay rent. I tried to pay rent and they would not let me. I stayed faithful in paying the amount I committed to pay to the missionaries. The stretching in giving came when God had me give money away while visiting ministry functions. Numerous times God had me give all the money I had in my wallet at ministry functions leaving not knowing how I was going to make it. God was faithful each time I was obedient to follow the Holy Spirit's prompting to give money away. Each time I was obedient to give my last amount of money away at ministry functions God provided for me within the next few days. It went against logic almost every time.

One example of me giving all the money I had left of faith came when God had me donate $200 dollars to a ministry on a Saturday. The money was all I had saved up at the time and I had bills due the following week. I stepped out in faith and gave the $200 to the ministry as the Holy Spirit prompted me to. In my mind, I was thinking I have no idea how I am going to make it or pay my bills. Giving the money away went completely against logic because I had bills due that I thought I was not going to be able to pay. I returned to work Monday and I made close to $100 dollars in tips two days in a row which was the most money I ever received in tips. God knew in advance what was going to happen the following week when He prompted me to give all the money I had saved up away. God has already seen beginning to the end and nothing takes God by surprise. Revelation 1:8 (NASB) states "I am the Alpha and the Omega," says the Lord God, "who is and who was and who is to come, the Almighty". Psalm 139:16 (NASB) states "Your eyes have seen my unformed substance; And in Your book, were all written the days that were ordained *for me*, when as yet there was not one of them". We are living out a life that God has seen from beginning to the end. When God asks us step out in faith in giving, He has already seen the other side of it and knows how our provision will come to us if we are obedient to follow the promptings of the Holy Spirit. God provided for me when I stepped out in faith in giving.

Another example of God having me step out faith in giving during this time occurred while I was at church service on a Sunday morning. The Sunday morning was a little different because I had plans to attend a concert later that night. I had a set amount of money held back in my wallet to pay for gas and parking at the concert later that night. While at the church service, the Holy Spirit prompted me to give the money I had set aside for the concert to a friend. I had not put gas in my truck yet and the gas tank was literally on empty at church. In my mind, I was thinking "if I give him this money, then I have no way to pay for gas to drive to the concert". I was obedient to give what the Holy Spirit prompted me to give which was all the money I had set aside to go to the concert. When church service ended, a random person asked me to take them to the store. I never told them I did not have money or did not have gas. I simply gave them a ride contemplating in my mind how I was going to get money to get to the concert later that day. While at the store, the person randomly gave me the same amount of money I had set aside to go to the concert away earlier at church. God already knew what was going to happen when He asked me to give the money I had set aside for the concert away. He knew the person I was going to give a ride to was going to give me the money I needed before it happened. Once again, God provided when He asked me all the money I had set aside away.

The promptings to give in the previous examples came by God speaking it to directly to my heart. Each time I had an inner knowing it was God prompting me to give. The speaking was internal directly to my heart and definitely God. The speaking came directly to my heart inside my spirit and it did not go away each time I was prompted. I knew it was God because it would not go away. The prompting to give stayed inside my heart in my spirit until I was obedient. I gave out of obedience to God and love for the person. I also stood on the scriptures of sowing and reaping in giving. Although the fruit of sowing and reaping is not always manifested as quick as took place in these two examples, every time we sow in the kingdom we reap.

I knew inside to be obedient when God prompted me to give because God would provide. God had already given me a deep revelation of Him being in control and that He has seen all my days from the beginning to the end. As much as the giving denied logic, I had peace in giving the last amount of money because I had faith God would provide. Trust had been built in God by seeing Him move personally numerous times in my life. The timing is God's timing. Sometimes we reap quick and sometimes the reaping is not quick. Stepping out in giving takes faith and trust in God. You have to trust God will provide when you sow into others in giving and have enough faith to act in obedience when prompted by the Holy Spirit.

I have learned when God says to give to be obedient and give. Instant obedience works best. The more you think about it the harder it becomes to give especially if it is all you have left. According to the Bible, all money is God's anyways. Psalm 24:1 (NASB) states "The earth is the LORD'S, and all it contains, the world, and those who dwell in it". Once you get a deep revelation of everything on earth being God's, then giving the money away becomes easier because you realize it is not your own anyways. 1 Timothy 1:17-19 (NASB) states "Command those who are rich in this present world not to be arrogant nor to put their hope in wealth, which is so uncertain, but to put their hope in God, who richly provides us with everything for our enjoyment. Command them to do good, to be rich in good deeds, and to be generous and willing to share. In this way they will lay up treasure for themselves as a firm foundation for the coming age, so that they may take hold of the life that is truly life."

A deeper revelation to give is that once we die we go to heaven as stated in Matthew 6:19-21 (NASB) "Do not store up for yourselves treasures on earth, where moth and rust destroy, and where thieves break in and steal. But store up for yourselves treasures in heaven, where neither moth nor rust destroys, and where thieves do not break in or steal; for where your treasure is, there your heart will be also".

When God prompts us to give and we are obedient we are building our home in heaven. As Christians, we should live with a heavenly mindset being fully obedient to God's will and His promptings to us by the Holy Spirit. Colossians 3:1-4 (NASB) states "Therefore if you have been raised up with Christ, keep seeking the things above, where Christ is, seated at the right hand of God. Set your mind on the things above, not on the things that are on earth. For you have died and your life is hidden with Christ in God. When Christ, who is our life, is revealed, then you also will be revealed with Him in glory". The closer you grow to God the more you realize your time on earth is to build your home in heaven. 2 Corinthians 4:18 (NASB) states "while we look not at the things which are seen, but at the things which are not seen; for the things which are seen are temporal, but the things which are not seen are eternal". Do not give to build a home but give out of love for God and for the person you are giving to. Any other motive would be wrong, and God knows anyways.

Besides the two examples listed above, God stretched me in giving at work as well. Numerous times I felt in my spirit to give my daily tip money to my coworkers. Each time I felt the unction of the Holy Spirit to give I gave to my coworkers. They never asked for money or said they needed money. The Holy Spirit simply prompted me to give. One-time God told me to give money to a coworker who needed the money for gas, but he never told anyone he needed money. Another time God told me to give money to a girl who needed the money to pay her bills. Her grandmother was sick, and they were behind on bills. She never asked for help or told anyone. Numerous times the Holy Spirit prompted me to put money in her car or give it to her directly. The unction's to give to her were a weekly occurrence. Each time I was obedient. One time she broke down crying thanking me because the money God had me give to her helped pay bills she was behind on. She was literally in tears weeping thanking me for being obedient to God. I simply followed the promptings of the Holy Spirit and opened up her car door or threw it inside her rolled down window. One thing I have learned is to be obedient to the promptings of the Holy Spirit because God delights in it. I probably gave the girl around a $1000 over a six-month time period. I knew to be obedient to God even though I needed the spending money myself. 1 Samuel 15:22 (NASB) states "Samuel said, "Has the LORD as much delight in burnt offerings and sacrifice as in obeying the voice of the LORD? Behold, to obey is better than sacrifice, *And* to heed than the fat of rams".

Before I lost the job, God did a miracle in provision. When I started the job, I had an older Honda I drove which was not the best. It was reliable at first, but the car kept having engine problems. During this time, I was traveling between Tennessee and North Carolina to see my son frequently. The car started giving me trouble by burning oil and blowing spark plugs. The car would not keep oil and would overheat blowing the spark plugs. It was not a pleasant experience because the upkeep was getting expensive.

One time on the way to see my son the car died about an hour outside of Charlotte. I managed to drive the car to a mechanic only to be told the car would not run much longer. I drove the car back to Charlotte and when I got back it was dead to the point of not running anymore. I cranked the engine and the engine did not turn over. A previous time the car had acted up similarly to where it would not start. At this point in life, I was surrounded by strong believers in faith. I told my roommate the car would not start and he asked, "did you pray for it". I told him yes, but he could pray for it as well. I had literally been trying to get it to start for 30 mins to an hour. The car had burned up all the oil, and I was pretty sure the engine was locked up completely. A couple of borderline mechanics I talked to came to the same conclusion.

My roommate came outside and laid hands on the car. He prayed "In the name of Jesus I pray this car runs" and he told me to start it up. I got in the car, put the key in the ignition and it cranked right up. I never had a bit of trouble out of it again until a few months later when it died completely. God restored my car from the dead literally like Lazarus. John 11:40-44 (NASB) states "Then Jesus said, "Did I not tell you that if you believe, you will see the glory of God?" So they took away the stone. Then Jesus looked up and said, "Father, I thank you that you have heard me. I knew that you always hear me, but I said this for the benefit of the people standing here, that they may believe that you sent me." When he had said this, Jesus called in a loud voice, "Lazarus, come out!" The dead man came out, his hands and feet wrapped with strips of linen, and a cloth around his face". Similar to Lazarus, Jesus rose the car back from the dead which was a miracle.

Now that the car was dead, my back against the wall. I only had about $1000 saved up at the time. A men's conference was coming up I wanted to attend but did not have the extra money to go to it. I was praying for God to provide to go to the conference. A few Sunday's later after praying, a friend came to me and said, "God told me to pay your way to the conference and you should look into going". The conference occurred within a couple of weeks of the car dying. I took the offer and went to the conference. On the way back from the conference, I was riding with a person explaining to him that I was looking for a new car that mine had died. I told him the story of what happened to the car.   During a period of silence in our conversation, the Holy Spirit spoke to me "I am going to provide a truck for you". I kind of brushed it off and continued to look for a car after returning home from the men's conference.

I kept asking God if it was His will to provide a car for me doubting the word that was spoken to me by Him. Needless to say, I lived in unbelief not standing on the word that was spoken to my spirit by God about Him providing a truck for me and I found a car I could afford. I called to check on the car and made arrangements to get it. On a Thursday morning, I prayed to God telling Him if it is not your will for me to get this car then stop it. Not long after saying the prayer I received a random phone call. The call was short and straight to the point. When I picked up the phone and answered it this is what I heard on the other end "God told me to buy you a truck. You are not to worry about buying a car. I found one at a car lot and they are getting it ready for you to drive. We will go pick it up Saturday after the prayer meeting if that is ok with you. God bless you." At this point, I had tears of joy and was thanking God.

God performed a miracle in my life in the form of provision. God provided a truck like He told me He would do. When God gives a prophetic word, we can count on Him to be faithful to fulfill it. Jeremiah 1:12 (NASB) states "Then the LORD said to me, "You have seen well, for I am watching over My word to perform it" and Isaiah

55:11 (NASB) states" So will My word be which goes forth from My mouth; It will not return to Me empty, Without accomplishing what I desire, And without succeeding *in the matter* for which I sent it". When God speaks a Rhema prophetic word in our life we can be certain He will be faithful to fulfill it. We have to stand in faith and not let unbelief creep in until it comes to pass in the natural.

Being Spirit led

At this point in the book, I am going to branch out from living on faith in the form of provision to being led by the spirit daily. Once you are accustomed to hearing God's voice speaking to your spirit, He will lead you daily. This chapter will center on being led by the Spirit. Romans 8:14 (NASB) states "For all who are being led by the Spirit of God, these are sons of God." John 3:8 (NASB) states "The wind blows where it wishes and you hear the sound of it, but do not know where it comes from and where it is going; so is everyone who is born of the Spirit." The spirit led life can be a somewhat odd life, but it assures you are a child of God because His spirit living inside you is leading you as long as you are walking in the light freely confessing sins when you commit them.

The second verse is listed here to emphasize when being led by the spirit you have no idea how your day will go. The more I follow God the more of a reality the verse becomes to me. One time I took my friend to take his trash off and the trip literally took around 2 hours. While driving to the gas station the Holy Spirit prompted me to stop and encourage a guy on a bicycle. God put it heavy on my heart to pray for provision for him. As I approached him and told him what God told me about provision the word was spot on. Me and my friend prayed for him and even got to see the fruit of prayer as it was answered. After successfully taking the trash off and praying for more people, we saw a car stop and give the guy on the bike money that we prayed for earlier on our way back home. It is great to see God move and to be used by God. The normal trash taking of 30 mins literally took almost 2 hours as we were led to minister to people on the side of the street while driving.

Another example of being led by the Spirit is when I was at a Friday night worship service. While at the service the Holy Spirit prompted me to leave service early. Out of obedience I left when I was prompted. While I was driving down the road, I was thinking about where to buy groceries because I needed food. The Holy Spirit prompted me to go to Wal-Mart. After initially arguing with God not wanting to go to Wal-Mart, out of obedience I went to Wal-Mart. While at Wal-Mart I knew I was there on assignment from God. As I was walking down the drink aisle the Holy Spirit prompted me to talk to a lady. While talking to her God told me she was suffering from depression which was rooted in family issues stemming from addiction. Needless to say, the word was spot on. She opened up and told me about her nephew who was in jail and I was led to give her my testimony. The obedience to leave the worship service ended up opening up a door for me to minister in the jail to her nephew which I went into the jail and ministered to him via video for a season of his life. I was simply led by the Spirit and obedient when God led.

A third example of being led by Spirit occurred when I was needing to buy oil for my car. I was literally driving down the road about to stop and get oil for the car because it was a burning oil and almost out of oil. While driving and deciding where to buy oil, the Holy Spirit told me to wait. Out of obedience, I went home and waited. The next morning, I woke up and was praying and remembered I needed to get oil. I got up got dressed and the Holy Spirit told me to leave at 9:30. I sat back down and journaled what God gave me. I asked God where He wanted me to go get oil at 9:30 and I had an open vision of the Dollar General store. At 9:30 I leave to go to the Dollar General store. While there, I got behind a person in line and God told me to tell them Jesus loved them and prayed for them. Being obedient, I approached him in the parking lot and told him Jesus loves him and pray for him. The guy had been going through a hard time and was about to give up on both God and life. He had been praying for God to send someone to minister to him that morning before going to the store. I was the answer to his prayer.

These are just a few of the many examples of being led by Holy Spirit. Basically, when I go about my day, I listen to the inner promptings of the Holy Spirit to guide me and I step into faith. The

Bible states in Psalm 118:24 (NASB) "This is the day which the LORD has made; Let us rejoice and be glad in it". God has made the whole day for us. We simply have to ask Him what good works He has prepared for us to do on that day and obey when He speaks to our hearts. The promptings of the Holy Spirit are spoken straight to our heart. The prompting is an inner voice that sounds like our own that starts from the inside and moves outward. The more time you spend with God, the more you will know the voice of the Holy Spirit. The ability to discern His promptings come from time spent in private listening and distinguishing His voice from our own and the enemies and stepping out in faith. Luke 16:10 (NASB) states "He who is faithful in a very little thing is faithful also in much; and he who is unrighteous in a very little thing is unrighteous also in much". If you can be faithful in the little things as the Holy Spirit prompts you, then you can be faithful in the bigger things as God gives them to you. Basically, I learned by sitting and being quiet asking God questions and writing down what God gave me.

Building blocks of faith

You may be asking yourself did I just wake up with the faith level I am showing in this book. The answer is no. God gives different measures of faith. Romans 12:3 (NASB) "For through the grace given to me I say to everyone among you not to think more highly of himself than he ought to think; but to think so as to have sound judgment, as God has allotted to each a measure of faith". We are all on our own journey with faith. I do not have a magical answer on how God gives faith, but I do know from my own experience faith can be built up in a person. Paul quoted in 2 Corinthians 10:14 – 16 (NASB)"For we are not overextending ourselves, as if we did not reach to you, for we were the first to come even as far as you in the gospel of Christ; not boasting beyond *our* measure, *that is*, in other men's labors, but with the hope that as your faith grows, we will be, within our sphere, enlarged even more by you, so as to preach the gospel even to the regions beyond you, *and* not to boast in what has been accomplished in the sphere of another" which shows faith can grow along with sphere of influence. Also, Romans 10:17 (NASB) states "So faith *comes* from hearing, and hearing by the word of Christ" which means we get faith by hearing the word.

Now, I will give testimonies of how God built faith in my own life using personal testimonies of what God has done in my life and through me. I rededicated my life to Jesus at Teen Challenge Ministry. I was a suicidal drug addict for almost 15 years. Teen Challenge is the vessel God used to change my life and to start building my faith. While at Teen Challenge, God used different events to build my faith and trust in Him. During the time I was at Teen Challenge, I had to memorize scripture, read the Bible, and read books pertaining to God along with listening to sermons in chapels. God used the testimonies of healing that were being told to me by my minsters to plant seed in me to build faith. Most of the testimonies I heard were associated with healing, deliverance, family restoration, and court cases being dropped because I was in a ministry associated with deliverance. Most of the men in the ministry were facing serious life controlling issues along with jail or prison sentences.

God was using my ministers to plant seed about healings in other people's lives. The testimonies I was listening to were planting seed in me to build my faith. Just like Romans 10:17 (NASB) says "So faith *comes* from hearing, and hearing by the word of Christ". Also, being in the Word daily reading it was building faith in me reading the stories in the Bible. Being engulfed in the Bible and hearing testimonies was the first building block God used in my life to build my faith. After the seed of testimonies and Bible reading was planted in me, God started answering prayers in my life to build my faith. I knew to pray, believe, and expect what I was praying into according to God's will. While I was in Teen Challenge Ministry, I started seeing prayers answered, some instantly, which built my faith.

A few examples God used during this time to build faith are listed here to show you how God built my faith. One example of a healing prayer getting answered occurred when I contracted Hepatitis C from injecting up drugs and sharing needles. The virus at the time was incurable. One night we went to a healing and miracle service in Hot Springs, Arkansas on a Friday night. While there, the lady ministering stated she had been used to heal incurable diseases. I had been praying for deliverance to this incurable virus since I found out I was diagnosed with it and I knew this was God's answer to my prayer. When I went up for prayer, I knew God was going to heal me. I was the first person in line and never even told her what I wanted prayer for. She literally had eyes that looked right though me and told me to have in my spirit what I wanted prayer for when I came forward. I was already thanking God for the healing and could feel God's presence all around her. Before she even touched me to pray for me, I fell out in the Spirit and was laid out on the ground for a few minutes. The next time I went to get tested for Hepatitis C the doctor called me and told me the virus was still in me, but the virus was dead. He had no explanation except I was a lucky man and I responded to him "God is good."

Another prayer God answered instantly was when I contracted poison ivy from working in the woods. The poison ivy came up and started itching. I immediately recognized what it was, and I laid my hand where it was at on my ankle and asked God to take away the itching along with the rash. After the prayer, the itching subsided and the next morning the poison ivy rash was completely gone. God healed the poison ivy allergic reaction and built my faith. Another time God built my faith at Teen Challenge by answering prayer occurred when I ran out of toothpaste. The morning I ran out I never told anyone I ran out. While at Teen Challenge you do not have the privilege to go to the store. You basically have no freedom except what the ministry offers. I got on my hands and knees and prayed to God for toothpaste. Later that day, I got the privilege to go to the store with a staff member after a odd day of divinely orchestrated circumstances and got to buy toothpaste. God answered my prayer and built my faith. Once you learn God's ways you can start to see His hand throughout your day in answering your prayers which will build your faith.

The previous listed testimonies are very few of the many answered prayers that God used to build my faith. I have seen God answer so many prayers it would be exhausting to list them all here. Hopefully, you understand the concept and pattern of God's building blocks of faith in answering prayers.

Forced to trust God

Up until this point in my walk with God, I thought I had trust in God. I had shelter provided for me, I had food provided for me, and I had seen God's hand in provision a few different times in my life. I honestly thought my trust in God had reached full capacity. I walked around with my head high evangelizing thinking to myself "I fully trust God". God was about to force me to trust Him in a deeper way though. At my workplace, I had a manager who treated employees bad who took over the job site, and it was doing more damage than good to my spirit. God told me to turn in my 2 weeks' notice at the job and I did not do it. I convinced myself I was mishearing from God because it made no sense at all to quit the job. Two weeks from the day God told me to turn in my two weeks' notice at the job I got fired from it. God forced me into a deeper season of trust, and I learned I should have been obedient when God told me to be obedient to quit the job.

I lost the job because I ministered to a corporate lady by means of writing a letter and I got fired for it. The corporation said I was a security threat to them by placing the letter on the desk. I saw it as God removing me from the work place. The Holy Spirit told me to write the letter and I was obedient. I look back and see God's hand was all in it now and laugh at it. When I lost the job, I did not have much money in savings, and it was the middle of November. I knew God was calling me to take counseling classes at Liberty University when I got fired from the job. Besides pursuing taking classes at Liberty University with a little savings money, all I had to live on was faith in God.

Upon losing the job, I went to apply for food stamps and while getting the application the Holy Spirit spoke to me "Don't apply for food stamps". I walked in disobedience to the Holy Spirit and filled out the application. The prompting from the Holy Spirit never left and continued to grow stronger so I never turned in the application for food stamps. Everyone wants to see God move in their lives and for God to stretch them, but in order to have God move and be stretched you have to be in a position were God can do it. God desires a willing and obedient person as states in Isaiah 1:19-20 (NASB) "If you are willing and obedient, you shall eat the good of the land; but if you refuse and rebel, you shall be eaten by the sword; for the mouth of the LORD has spoken". I was obedient not to turn in the food stamp application, and I was fully in a position where I had to trust God and live on faith. I had no job, no money, no support from the government, and very little family support at the time.

I thought I had faith and trust in God, but when I was forced into a position with my back against the wall with nothing but God to rely on the truth came out. My faith in God was wavering and I was being doubleminded. I kept asking myself how I am going to make it. I started warring with scripture and standing on the truth realizing God was my only source for provision. Either God was going to provide for me, or I was going to die. Ephesians 6:18 (NASB) states "Therefore put on the full armor of God, so that when the day of evil comes, you may be able to stand your ground, and after you have done everything, to stand" and 1 Corinthians 6:13 (NASB) states "Be on the alert, stand firm in the faith, act like men, be strong". When we are in a position when we can do nothing else, we are to stand on the word of God and its promises.

I knew to stand on God's promises. God had moved enough in my life already and I had some faith built up. The emotional side of me wanted to panic. We should speak of things as though they are even though they are not. Just like the example given in Joel. Joel 3:10 (NASB) states "Beat your plowshares into swords and your pruning hooks into spears let the weak say, "I am a mighty man". The weak are supposed to claim they are strong and those who need provision should state they already have what God promises them they will have in the Bible. The Bible states God provides our needs so I started proclaiming and thanking God for His provision even though I did not have it yet following the example of Abraham in Romans 4:19-20 (NASB) which states "Without becoming weak in faith he contemplated his own body, now as good as dead since he was about a hundred years old, and the deadness of Sarah's womb; yet, with respect to the promise of God, he did not waver in unbelief but grew strong in faith, giving glory to God".

I was about to see God move in my life in a mighty way on a journey of faith which started because of the loss of a job. I steadily applied for jobs for the next 18 months and had interviews with companies, but God shut the door to all the potential job opportunities. It was one of the strangest things I have ever been through, but I recognized it as God shutting the door. I have a prophet friend I listened to weekly at this time who gave me a word saying, "God is shutting the doors on purpose to build discernment and spiritual strength for a later time in life". In other words, I was in a tough season of preparation.

December 2015

I had enough money in the bank to make it to December, and I was supposed to attend a conference in Kansas City at the end of December. I completely ran out of money about mid-December. All my plans for the conference seemed to have fallen through. I knew God called me to attend it and I had already purchased a ticket to the conference, I had no way to pay for food, transportation, and lodging. I made arrangements to see my son on Christmas day then planned to stay with friends in another part of Missouri close to where the conference was being held, but God had different plans. Because I lost my job, I did not have enough money to travel to see my son and stay with my friends. Instead, I was left praying to God and thanking Him in faith for the miraculous provision for the trip even though it had not happened yet. When I ran out of money right before Christmas, I was completely out of gas and food along with all necessities at one point. I needed help I prayed to God saying, "I know you are provider and I trust You to provide". The next day, I got a check in the mail un-expectantly which was enough to buy everything I needed. God answered my prayer and provided by sending a check in the mail.

It was mid-December now and I knew God was still leading me to attend the conference at the end of December. The money from the previous check I received in the mail diminished. I prayed to God again because I needed food and gas. I received another random check in the mail which covered all my gas and food a second time. The check was completely random. I got in my truck to leave to a ministry and the Holy Spirit told me to check the mailbox before I left. Out of obedience I did and inside the mailbox was another unexpected check, but I still did not have money to go to the conference. God had faithfully provided all my food, gas, and necessities for a solid month since I lost my job with random checks in the mail, but I still could not afford to go the conference.

A couple days before I was supposed to leave for the conference, I got a text from a friend saying someone dropped out of their riding arrangements and I could ride for free with them if I wanted to. I still had no money saved up for the conference because I was not working. I was applying for jobs and having interviews, but each time God shut the door. God provided a ride to the conference, but I still had no money to pay for food when I got there. The night before the conference I was at a worship service and another friend told me not to worry about paying for food while at the conference because God told him to cover all of my food expenses without me ever asking anyone for help. God provided for the rest of the way to the conference after I stepped out in faith and bought the ticket.

When we left to drive to the conference, I had very little money and no gas in my truck when we left from Charlotte, NC to Kansas City, MO. The gas light was on in my truck when we left for Kansas City, and I was going to have to buy gas to drive home when we returned to Charlotte. While at the conference God provided for all my meals and, God put it on someone's heart to pay for my lodging as well. While at the conference, God had me give what little money I had to support a ministry. I was thinking when I get back to Charlotte, I have no way to get home because the truck was out of gas when we left. On the drive back to Charlotte, someone randomly handed me gas money without me ever asking or telling anyone I needed gas money. The group had extra money left over from the trip and God put it on the person's heart to give me their excess money. Once again, God provided every step of the way for the conference and gas money to get home. I stepped out in faith and bought a ticket when God provided the rest.

New season: Liberty classes

January 2016

After returning to Charlotte from the conference in Kansas City, a new season started in my life along with a new year. I received Christmas money in the mail while at the conference which helped cover food and gas for a few weeks until once again I was out of money. I found myself positioned with my back against the wall again praying to God not knowing what to do. I was supposed to help a ministry and I needed gas to get there. To my surprise, I got a check in the mail from a car insurance company. To this day I am still clueless as to what the check was for from the insurance company. The check had no explanation or letter attached to it. It was simply a check wrote out to me. God did a miracle in provision and the check provided for all of my needs. The insurance check provided money for a few weeks then I was on my knees praying to God again.

I was learning to trust God and seeing His faithfulness in my life. When random checks come in the mail for close to two months straight, exactly when you need them it really starts to boost your faith. The miraculous provision helps remove the if's, and's, and but's from your thought process. The what ifs become more walking faith knowing God will provide what you ask Him for when you need it. It was getting close to the end of January. My diet at this time was mostly beans and rice. Not the best of food but appropriate when you are living a sacrificed life. The diet of mostly beans and rice allowed me to spend more money on gas than food. I still gave money away when prompted by the Holy Spirit, but the amount was mostly small amounts given at church services. Close to the end of January, I was out of gas and praying to God because I needed gas to get to church. I remember a Saturday night I was sitting at home with the gas light on in my truck. I received a text message not long after praying saying meet me at the gas station up the road from your house. God put it on a gentlemen's heart to buy gas and I never asked him. Once again, God supernaturally provided for me. All I did was pray to Him.

It is easy to take the American culture for granted and spoil yourself with commodities not even realizing it. Living a life of sacrifice to God is what Jesus did. Mark 10:45 (NASB) states "For even the Son of Man did not come to be served, but to serve, and to give His life a ransom for many ". Paul stated it well in 1 Corinthians 15:31 (NASB) stating "I affirm, brethren, by the boasting in you which I have in Christ Jesus our Lord, I die daily". When you live the sacrificed life, you may be exposed to live in some humble circumstances. The Bible says to boast in our humble circumstances. James 1:9-10 (NASB) states "But the brother of humble circumstances is to glory in his high position; and the rich man is to glory in his humiliation, because like flowering grass he will pass away".

In our humility, we learn to thank God for providing our food and clothing no matter what form the food provision comes in. God knows everything going on in our lives better than we do, and He will provide our food for us we just have to be content when He provides it. Paul stated it well saying, "If we have food and covering, with these we shall be content" in 1 Timothy 6:8 (NASB). Also, Paul stated in Philippians 4:11-13 (NASB) "Not that I speak from want, for I have learned to be content in whatever circumstances I am. I know how to get along with humble means, and I also know how to live in prosperity; in any and every circumstance I have learned the secret of being filled and going hungry, both of having abundance and suffering need. I can do all things through Him who strengthens me". When you love God, you will go to all measures to obey Him because you love Him so much. You realize the humble circumstances are nothing in light of eternity which is coming after earth. 2 Corinthians 4:16-18 (NASB) states "Therefore we do not lose heart, but though our outer man is decaying, yet our inner man is being renewed day by day. For momentary, light affliction is producing for us an eternal weight of glory far beyond all comparison, while we look not at the things which are seen, but at the things which are not seen; for the things which are seen are temporal, but the things which are not seen are eternal".

February 2016

January came to an end and I had survived another month living off faith alone. I was still applying for jobs, but God kept shutting the door on them. I was staying busy with school at Liberty during this time studying counseling classes. I was learning a lot about God beyond just provision during this time. I learned more about His mercy, grace, forgiveness, patience, and understanding when we fall short of the mark living a holy life. There were a few times early in this faith walk my behavior was far short of what a Christian should have been. I found myself looking back at the past 3 months realizing God's provision in a real way. My diet was still mostly beans, rice, and oatmeal. God still had me fasting quite a bit as well during this season with 3 days and 21 days fast. I was truly learning to live a sacrificed life as God led me.

February took a little different turn. I was staying at home more because of the excessive amount of school work. I walked to the grocery store because it was literally a ten-minute walk from where I lived at. Rent was still free. I offered to pay for rent, but the owners insisted I stayed there for free and would not take any money from me. Most of my gas money was used to help out in ministries because I was active in ministries and church groups. I received a couple of unexpected checks in the mail again in February which helped pay for food and gas. I was not driving much so I did not use an excess of gas.

One night during February an unexpected event happened which drove me to my knees. The event was random and a learning lesson. I parked my truck on the side of the road just like I had for the whole previous year. I woke up the next morning to drive to a prayer meeting and my truck was not where I had parked it. I was concerned someone had stolen my truck. There was no indication of anything happening to my truck like it being towed. I prayed for a minute before I called the police to tell them my car had been stolen. My neighbor at the time came outside and I asked him if he knew anything about what happened to my truck. He asked if I checked to see if the truck had been towed. There were tow laws that were just starting to be enforced and the tow truck chose my truck to tow out of all the other cars parked illegally. I called the tow truck company and I did not have the money to get it out. The tow bill was close to two hundred dollars. I prayed to God telling Him I had no way to get the truck out of the tow lot, which He was already aware of.

Not long after praying, the Holy Spirit started speaking to me showing me how this whole event was divinely set up by God. I started to develop a heavenly mindset towards it realizing there was a higher purpose to my truck being towed. It started to make sense that only my truck was towed out of all the numerous cars parked illegally and that it had not been towed almost the whole previous year. Along with the change in thought process, someone randomly offered to pay the bill and drove me to the place where the truck was being held. I never asked anyone to pay the bill. God put it on their heart to pay it without me asking. My friend simply said" thank God buddy".

While driving to get the truck out of the car pound, I told my friend there is a higher purpose to this. When we got to the car pound there was a guy there getting his car out too and I started flowing prophetically speaking into his life. I do not remember all of the words exactly, but I do know he broke down in tears crying and was amazed at the words being spoken to him because they were spot on. I realized God had divinely orchestrated the whole event for me to minister to the guy at the car pound and God supernaturally provided for the whole incident.

Most of February I was at home doing college work and did not use much money. Close to the end of February on a

Wednesday night I was needing gas money to get to a ministry I helped with. I prayed to God telling Him I needed money to get to the ministry. I was at the house by myself waiting thinking to myself how God was going to provide for me to get to the ministry. I was sitting outside on the porch praying and meditating on God when my roommate pulled up. He got out his car asked how I was doing and said you need gas money to get to the ministry and handed me the money. I never told him I needed the money to get to the ministry. He just told me to thank God for it, and I was able to make it to the ministry. As you can see, I never asked people for help. I simply prayed to God each time I needed money. The bible says in 1 Peter 5:6-7 (NASB) "humble yourselves under the mighty hand of God and in due time He will exalt you casting all of your cares on Him because He cares for you". I truly believe we are supposed to go to God with everything and not ask for help from anyone but God.

March 2016

February came to an end, and I had survived two and a half months completely living on faith in God. I was not asking for help from people or family. A lot of my time was consumed with college work. The transition into college kept me busy with reading and writing research papers. I still helped out at the abortion clinic when I was led. One morning in March I was out of money and wanted something to drink besides water. I got on my hands and knees and prayed to God telling Him I wanted something besides water to drink. He immediately put it on my heart to go to the abortion clinic. It was a Saturday morning and this day there was an outreach going on there, so I drove to it and walked up to the clinic. A strange event happened while walking along the sidewalk. One of the participants at the abortion clinic accidentally cut himself and I offered him a ride to the restroom to clean the cut. He preferred to go to a gas station instead. While in the gas station, he bought me a drink. God faithfully answered my prayer to have something to drink that morning besides water. I just had to be obedient and drive to the abortion clinic.

The Bible states not to worry about food because God will provide for our food. When we pray for God to provide for our food, we do not know how He will answer it. Isaiah 55:8-9 (NASB) "For My thoughts are not your thoughts, Nor are your ways My ways," declares the LORD. "For *as* the heavens are higher than the earth, So are My ways higher than your ways And My thoughts than your thoughts." We try to limit God and box God. God can move and work in ways way beyond what we can comprehend. God provided food for Jesus in miracles. Matthew 14:13-21 (NASB) states "Now when Jesus heard *about John*, He withdrew from there in a boat to a secluded place by Himself; and when the people heard *of this*, they followed Him on foot from the cities. When He went ashore, He saw a large crowd, and felt compassion for them and healed their sick. When it was evening, the disciples came to Him and said, "This place is desolate and the hour is already late; so send the crowds away, that they may go into the villages and buy food for themselves." But Jesus said to them, "They do not need to go away; you give them *something* to eat!" They *said to Him, "We have here only five loaves and two fish." And He said, "Bring them here to Me." Ordering the people to sit down on the grass, He took the five loaves and the two fish, and looking up toward heaven, He blessed *the food*, and breaking the loaves He gave them to the disciples, and the disciples *gave them* to the crowds, and they all ate and were satisfied. They picked up what was left over of the broken pieces, twelve full baskets. There were about five thousand men who ate, besides women and children".

During this time, most of my meals were consistently rice and beans. Only on rare occasions did I stray from eating beans and rice. The sacrificed life is not easy, but you learn a lot about yourself and God if you do it. God will bless you and surprise you while giving you the desires of your heart and the things you don't ask for. An example of God providing food in the ways of a miracle I did not ask for is stated here to build your faith. God provided food for me through another person's job in the form of a miracle when I had no money to buy food. I was on my hands and knees praying to God for food because I had no food or money. The timing was about the middle of March. I was spending most of my money on gas to go evangelism outreaches and the abortion clinic during this time. I did not eat out much during this time period besides beans, rice, and oatmeal. Let me remind you I live a sacrificed life. During this time period, I sacrificed premium food and ate mostly beans and rice. I never said living by faith would provide you with the finest things. I simply said God is faithful. 2 Corinthians 5:7 (NASB) states "Walk by faith not by sight". My soul ambition was to seek God wholeheartedly and do college work.

I had a friend who worked for a large corporation and the corporation had a banquet multiple days the same week I prayed for food. The banquet was catered by a food company which took a head count of the number people attending to know exactly how much food to bring. Somehow the corporation miscounted the number of people and ordered excess food and gave the extra food to my roommate. The excess food came in the form of complete boxed lunches. The mishap was a big mishap because I received 4 complete lunches along with other meals that were left at the corporation. I recognized it as God providing for me. To make it better instead of just being a onetime provision it happened multiple times the same week which my roommate said had never happened before and the corporation had no explanation for it. A couple days later I was brought 4 more complete box lunches because of another miscalculation by the corporation. I see it as God providing. Like most corporations this one was concerned about money, so the mishap was not planned in any way. God provided a miracle in the form of food by providing me with complete box lunches which lasted me a week from my roommate's workplace. God is good.

I received a couple more checks in the mail which helped provide for the gas to get to ministry functions. God also had random people hand me money. I never asked for help at any point in this faith walk. I simply prayed to God when I needed something. A few times I was ministering at life group functions and random people would hand me money. They would simply say "God told me to give this to you'. I also attended prayer meetings regularly during this time. One-time God led me to a prayer meeting; I got there, walked in, and a lady went to her wallet, pulled out money, and handed it to me saying, "God knows what you need". Another time I woke up and did not have enough gas to get to church so I prayed telling God I needed money to drive to church. About an hour later, my roommates asked me if I was going to church and I told them yes then they handed me twenty dollars telling me to use it to get there. I never asked for the money.

March was about to come to a close and I had successfully survived another month living only on faith. The life was sacrificed. I spent my time doing school work, ministry work, and seeking God. Most of my free time was used either spreading the gospel or in intimacy with God. My heart's desire is to always go deeper in God. To go deeper you have to be willing to be stretched. God was about to honor my prayer to go deeper in April and stretch me a little farther in my faith and giving level.

April 2016

It was the beginning of April, my diet of fasting, beans, rice, and oatmeal was sufficient for my health along with vitamins and occasional protein supplements. I was praying for God to take me deeper. You may be thinking you are already living off nothing but faith which I was, but I still wanted to go deeper in God. God was about to stretch me a little farther. I received grants to attend college and I was about to receive extra money back from school. I was wanting to attend a ministry during this time and was praying to God for the money to attend. The ministry was $950 to attend. I had half of the money and still needed around $400. I was praying God I need the money to attend this ministry. Around the beginning of April, I randomly checked the amount of money I was going to receive back from school. I got on the computer to check and to my surprise I received an extra $400 back. I had no idea why I was getting an extra $400 back so I checked into the grant. When I did more research about the grant, I realized I had randomly received another grant of $800 I never applied for. I have no idea where the grant money came from and it was applied to my account halfway through the semester. I recognized it as God providing the extra amount of money I needed.

In order to grow in God, you have to be willing to take risk and step out in faith. Stepping out in faith in God normally goes against logic. The thing to do when stepping out in faith is to not overthink what you are doing looking at the circumstances in the natural, and to completely trust in God being obedient to do what He is asking you to do. 1 Samuel 15:22 (NASB) states "Has the LORD as much delight in burnt offerings and sacrifices as in obeying the voice of the LORD? Behold, to obey is better than sacrifice, *And* to heed than the fat of rams". God will prompt you in the Holy Spirit letting you know what you need to do.

When you feel the prompting of the Holy Spirit to step out in faith in giving, praying, or giving a prophetic word be obedient to what God is telling you to do. God has seen everything from the beginning to the end of time so there is nothing to be scared of. Just trust what God is telling you to do and be obedient. David wrote in Psalm 139:16 (NASB) "Your eyes have seen my unformed substance; And in Your book were all written. The days that were ordained for me, when as yet there was not one of them". We have to remember God has already seen the future. He knows the beginning to the end of our lives. He knows everything. Nothing takes God by surprise. God is omnipotent. Psalm 147:4-5 (NASB) states "He counts the number of the stars; He gives names to all of them. Great is our Lord and abundant in strength; His understanding is infinite". I am emphasizing to not fear and to trust God has your future when you step out in faith.

You have to remember when we step out in faith in giving, that God knows the future and to trust Him. The more you put yourself in a position to be fully dependent on God the easier it becomes to trust God. Faith and trust in God will be built up in you by stepping out in faith and putting yourself in positions where you are completely dependent on God. You cannot grow without willing to be stretched. It is easy to put security in money and earthly things, but God wants us to be completely dependent on Him. In other words, to grow you have to be willing to give when God asks you to give. If you don't obey the promptings of the Holy Spirit, then God may not prompt you to give again which means you will not grow. The main principle behind stepping out in faith is trust. You have to trust God has your every need and will not lead you astray or harm you in any way. The more you step out in faith the easier it gets to do it.

Being fully reliant on God can be a lot easier said than done. It is easy to say, "oh yea I have faith and trust in God", but when you are forced into a position with your back against the wall the truth of where your faith and trust in God stand at will quickly rise to the surface. I cannot say this faith walk has been easy nor can I say I have not stumbled or gotten upset at God along the journey. I have learned a lot about mercy, grace, forgiveness, and the love of God during the process as well. I do say with confidence now "I know for a fact God always provides". Proverbs 10:3 (NASB) states "The LORD will not allow the righteous to hunger, But He will reject the craving of the wicked". God has stretched in giving and being fully reliant on Him to the point I know He is faithful to answer my prayers and provide as I wait on His hand to move in my life.

I wrote these past few paragraphs here to emphasize walking in obedience and trust in God over you own will. Now, back to the walking by faith journey. I had enough money saved up to attend the ministry I was wanting to attend. I was all set thinking to myself "alright I get to attend the ministry" until God prompted me to give all the money, I had saved up for the ministry away. I had close to $1000 and God told me to give the money to missionaries instead of attending the ministry. In October, I committed to giving to some different missionary families. God prompted me to give to the missionaries instead of attending the ministry and I had to make a decision. Out of obedience to God, I sacrificed attending the ministry and gave the money missionaries. The total amount I gave to the missionaries was around $800.

After giving the money to missionaries out of obedience to God, I was once again forced to live on faith because I gave away most of the money I had saved up at that time. I used the remaining money I had to buy food and gas. Not long after giving the money away, I was out of gas, food, and money again. I went to be alone with God at church to pray before attending a class and I needed provision. I knew God would make a way for me where it seemed like there was no way. I thanked God for His provision even though I did not have it in the natural yet. Less than five minutes later after praying at the church, someone handed me gas money and a food card without me ever asking or saying a word to them. They simply told me "God told me to give you this". God heard my prayer and provided.

Besides getting random checks in the mail and using people to provide, God will use jobs to provide as well. During this time period, I continued putting in job applications. I had interview after interview and kept getting told no. I realized God was shutting the door to the secular job world which was confirmed to me with prophetic words spoken into my life. Prophetic mentors spoke prophetically into my life telling me to trust God because He was doing a work in me that I would use later in life. The Bible states we are supposed to work in 2 Thessalonians 3:10-15 (NASB) states "For even when we were with you, we used to give you this order: if anyone is not willing to work, then he is not to eat, either. For we hear that some among you are leading an undisciplined life, doing no work at all, but acting like busybodies. Now such persons we command and exhort in the

Lord Jesus Christ to work in quiet fashion and eat their own bread. But as for you, brethren, do not grow weary of doing good. If anyone does not obey our instruction in this letter, take special note of that person¹and do not associate with him, so that he will be put to shame. *Yet* do not regard him as an enemy but admonish him as a brother".

Around the end of April, I was out gas, food, and money again which left me praying to God. Yet again, following day I got a call from someone to do computer work for them. Before I gave my life to Christ, I went to school for Information Technology and have multiple certifications in the field. The job was completely a one-day random job out of the blue I never applied for. I completed the job and did not ask for money when I completed the job. When I finished the job, I got paid enough to buy gas and food. I saw it as answered prayer. God put it on the person's heart to have me do their computer work for them right when I was in desperate need of money. My faith and trust in God were being built at an extraordinary rate. I was seeing supernatural provision happen right in front of my eyes. God provided for me living completely on faith for over five months straight as April came to an end.

May 2016

When the month of May started, I knew I was going to have to make a transition in living situations. The people I lived with were having a child, and I needed to be out of the house before the child was born. I was preparing myself for the transition not knowing how I was going make it. You have to remember I had not worked in almost 6 months and had no government help or help from family. I was truly living on faith in God. Most of my meals at this time were still rice and beans. At the beginning of May, I found myself on my hands and knees praying to God for food and gas. The common theme during this faith journey was running completely out of food and gas to see God come through and provide exactly when I needed Him to provide. God provided at the beginning of May with another random job after supplying the computer job. The next job came a couple weeks later when I got another random phone call to help a person move. God put it on the person's heart to have me help them move furniture. I drove a truck and they randomly called me one day asking for help and offering to pay me. The timing was perfect because I needed both food and gas money. God provided the answer to my prayer for food and gas in the form of a completely random job I never applied for exactly when I needed it. God is good.

After God provided the two random jobs, it was not long before I was out of gas and money again. The amount of money I was receiving was minimal and exactly what I needed to survive until I ran out again. God was supplying my needs just not in excess. I hit my knees again praying to God when I was in desperate need. Not long after praying I received a phone call to do another completely random one-day computer job I never applied for. The job paid for my food and gas. God was providing for me in the form of supernatural jobs I never applied for.

God answers our prayers, but sometimes not the way we think He will answer it. God's ways are higher than our ways we just have to trust Him when we pray to Him that He hears every word we speak and is faithful to answer what we ask Him to do. God's hand was in on providing the jobs. I never applied for any of them and provided the exact amount of money I needed exactly at the time I needed it. God made a way where there was no way.

The only problem with the jobs God was providing was that they were not supplying excess. The jobs were simply providing my needs for a short period of time and nothing more. I was still steadily eating beans, rice, and oatmeal at this part of the journey which was a sacrificed life. When the gas, food, and money ran out again I found myself on my knees praying to God for help. As you can see, living on faith keeps you on your knees close to God. Living a life fully reliant on God keeps you on your knees praying to God because He is your only source of provision. If you plan on trying or re-creating this faith walk journey, then be prepared because it was not an easy journey. My flesh rose up numerous times especially early in the walk when I was still learning God's ways and faithfulness. The longer the faith journey continued the more I trusted God to provide and the walk became easier. My faith level got to the point I knew God was going to provide in my life, I just did not know how He was going to do it. The questioning I had about God providing became an expectation of joy and excitement wondering how He was going to do it bringing a sense of wonder because I had no idea how it was going to manifest in the natural.

About this time in the journey, a ministry conference was coming up that I felt the Holy Spirit was leading me to attend. I hit my knees praying because I was in desperate need. God came to my rescue in the form of another random job. The job was another one day moving job. I had certain mentors who were looking out for me and set me up with a job behind the scenes. When God wants to bless you, He uses people. God will put people in your life anointed to bless you when He wants to bless you. I see it as God providing for me because I never asked them to get me the job. The job was offered to me randomly not long after praying for help. The job worked around the two colleges I was attending during this time and provided quite a bit of money. The amount of money I made in one day was more than I made at other jobs in a full week. God came through in my life in the form of provision by providing a moving job. The job was enough for me to pay all the bills I had due at the time as well as have extra money to attend the conference I felt led to attend.

While at the conference, attendees were prompted by the Holy Spirit to make a faith declaration in giving. The amount of money God put on my heart to give was $500 which seemed impossible for me to give at the time. I made the faith declaration to commit to giving $500 having no idea how I was going to come up with it only to remember that faith means God will provide it for me. In June, I got a random deposit of $500 into my bank account from an extra

$800 grant to pay for school that I have no idea where the grant money came from. The grant was randomly added to my college account and I never applied for it. The money was deposited to my bank account before the college was released to making deposits to student's bank accounts. God provided for me to give the $500 at the conference by supernaturally providing a grant and depositing the money early in my bank account. I simply stepped out in faith when God prompted me to give.

Other than working these few random jobs, God provided for me in different ways besides working during this season of life. I was offered two really good jobs, but I got prompted by the Holy Spirt not to take them. The Holy Spirit was prompting me very strong not to take either of the jobs which was not easy to do. It took me having faith in God telling the people no because they were both good jobs that were going to pay quite a bit of money. You have to remember by this time I had not worked in almost 7 months. I could have really used the money, but God told me not to take the jobs. I stepped out in faith telling the people no when my flesh was crying yes to take the job. My obedience to tell the people "No" even though I desperately needed the job took faith. It is hard to turn down a job when you are in dire need of provision. I was literally living week to week or day to day eating mostly rice and beans during this time. It was a sacrificing and humbling season.

I stood in faith and trust that I heard from God to tell the job offerors no and that God would provide for me in other ways. Romans 12:1-2 (NASB) states "Therefore I urge you, brethren, by the mercies of God, to present your bodies a living and holy sacrifice, acceptable to God, *which is* your spiritual service of worship. And do not be conformed to this world, but be transformed by the renewing of your mind, so that you may prove what the will of God is, that which is good and acceptable and perfect". The reason I told the people who offered me a job no is because I truly believed God had a plan for my life other than the two jobs offered. I did not have peace in my spirit in the decisions along with the strong promptings by the Holy Spirit to say no to them. When making tough decisions you should always follow peace as stated in Isaiah 55:12 (NASB) which states "For you will go out with joy and be led forth with peace; The mountains and the hills will break forth into shouts of joy before you, And all the trees of the field will clap *their* hands". Plus, I had enough faith and trust in God knowing He would provide for me fully.

June 2016

June came around and I had to make a transition. The couple I was living with was about to have a baby and I needed to be out of the house so they could start their family. I made arrangements for places to stay, but God shut the doors to all of them. I initially moved into a prayer house which was basically a church for two weeks asking God to give me a different place to stay. The first couple of days in the prayer house were difficult because I was not able to cook. The place had a refrigerator, bathroom, and sinks but had no stove or microwave to prepare food. I had to utilize what I had and make the best of what seemed a somewhat bad situation. I was helping teach a healing conference the first weekend of staying at the prayer house. I prayed for God to provide food for me before leaving to teach at the conference never telling anyone I needed help. The first night of the conference a lady brought me tacos to eat. She said God told her to bring me food. The second day of the conference another person took me out to eat saying God told them to take me to lunch. God provided food for me the first two days of the conference.

Saturday night after teaching the healing conference I went and dug into God. I still had no money, no gas, and no way to cook food. I got on my hands and knees and prayed to God to provide. Once again, He gave me the familiar scripture Isaiah 51 promising to make a way for me where there seemed no way at all. Sunday morning, I got up and drove to church questioning to myself how God was going to provide. I was an usher at the church I attended during this season of life. The head usher and I were close friends. On this Sunday morning, someone handed him complete meal tickets to a BBQ restaurant. He handed me two of the complete meal tickets. All I had to do to receive the food was go to the BBQ restaurant and give them the meal ticket. Before service someone came to me and asked if they could buy gas for me after church. I followed the person to the gas station after church service and they filled my truck up with gas. I never told a single person I needed anything. I went to God with it. God provided my needs fully all I had to do was wait and trust Him to move in my life.

I was only at the prayer house for a couple of weeks before I was offered another place to stay. The place I was offered would just be for the summer months but was free. They said they had extra room with a bed I was more than welcome to use it for free. God had provided another free place for me to stay. I was still in college full time which took most of my time. I spent my free time evangelizing, writing, or seeking God. I was still applying for jobs, but I was not even getting interviews. I changed my resume and was qualified for all the jobs I applied for. I still recognized it as God shutting the door. I realized He did not want me to work a secular job He was still preparing me for my future journey. I still had no income and was praying for food and gas money. The person I was living with helped with food when needed. I never spoke when I needed food, he simply provided for me.

God called me to a long fast during this summer and was faithful to provide exactly what I needed when I needed it. God told me to do a 40-day liquid fast to receive an impartation of wisdom and revelation and I was obedient. When God calls you to a fast there will be a grace on it. During this fast I did not get hungry. I do not recommend fasting unless led by the Holy Spirit and you contact a doctor first to determine whether you are healthy enough to perform the fast. The only time I fast is when God leads me to, and I adjust my exercise and bodily use accordingly. During the fast every time I ran out of milk, I prayed to God and He provided for me every single time I prayed. Each time I went to the prayer closet and told God what I needed and thanked Him for it in advance. Each time He sent someone with milk to the house or took me to the store and bought it. I never asked for help or told anyone I needed milk. God is so good just be obedient to His promptings.

I did not drive much during this time, so I was not using much gas. After the person filled my tank, it was sufficient for me to drive quite a long time. I started carpooling with my roommate which helped as well. I received more grant money back which provided money for gas. June came to an end with God supplying all my needs enough for each day. God says He will provide all your needs; He does not say it will be in excess though. My faith in God was built strong and I knew without a doubt God was going to provide for me I just didn't know how He was going to provide.

July 2016

July started and brought new challenges with it which required finances I did not have. I was living in Charlotte and my car tags expired. Most of my time was consumed doing school work. I was taking a heavy summer load to try to hurry up and finish my degree. I was still on the fast God called me to and still applying for jobs only to be told no. I realized God was keeping His hand on the job applications keeping the door shut to work. I spent my free time with God and spreading the gospel. I was connected to various evangelism teams and growing in the gifts God has given me. I was starting to grow more and step out more in the prophetic gifting's God had place in me, and I was still completely living on faith. I was learning God as provider with a deep personal revelation.

I knew when I got on my knees in the prayer closet God was going to give me what I asked for I just did not know the timing. During July, my car tags expired, and I prayed for a way to renew them. A few days later someone offered to pay for my car tags and mailed them to me. The other necessities I needed came once again

90

through random checks in the mail. Each time I needed money for necessities like toothpaste, shaving cream, razors and such things I prayed to God for them. One time in July I prayed when I needed them, and a few days later in the mail I received a money order in the mail without ever telling anyone what I needed. After the money from the money order ran out, I prayed to God again and I received a cashier's check from a bank. The cashier's check once again supplied for all my needs. I was still on the 40 day fast for most of the month of July. A couple more times I ran out of milk and I simply prayed to God for it. Both times I prayed, I received the milk I needed the exact same day with someone bringing it to me without telling them I needed it.

God provided provision another time in July with a weekend job. I was out of necessities and hit my knees praying to God. Within one day I received a random phone call from a lady I knew asking if I could dog sit for them while they went away on vacation. I saw the job as an answered prayer because the day before I was asking God to help me with my needs. In His faithfulness, He provided through a weekend job. I took the job and the money helped me survive for a couple more weeks. Remember most of my time was consumed with school work and I was not using much gas. I was eating mostly sandwiches and cheap quick fix food items during this time, but I had progressed from eating only beans and rice which was a blessing.

Nothing major happened in July. I was spending most of my time doing school work and my free time with God. One other testimony the Holy Spirit is prompting me to write about is when I needed a ride to a ministry on a Friday night. I was stuck one Friday with no way to go to a ministry I felt led to go to. I prayed to God in the prayer closet asking Him to provide a way for me to get to the ministry. I was offered a ride to the ministry from a person who had never been to the ministry before and has never been back since the night he took me. The person giving me a ride to the ministry was a onetime occurrence and answered prayer in my life. After the ministry, he took me out to eat and paid for it as well which was another answered prayer. As you can see, I learned to go to God with all my needs. July came to an end with God proving Himself faithful to provide for me in my life. July came to an end with me surviving another month living on faith alone. God is good.

August 2016

I moved out of the place I was staying in right before August. I transitioned back to the prayer house for a short season. My school schedule was extremely heavy, and I did not have much free time. I only told a few people that I was staying in the prayer house again. The few people I told all went to God with me in prayer. The great thing about being back at the prayer house was that it was close to everything and did not require much gas to get around. I was still connected with the evangelism team I was helping out before. I never once told them I needed anything, but God used them to provide in my life.

One time I met the evangelism team at the mall to do an outreach. Before leaving to the mall, I prayed to God because I did not have much gas. After the outreach was over, a person came and handed me $20 from the team. He simply said, "Brother Mike God knows what you need". The money was enough for me to get gas and food to last me until the weekend. Most of the food I was eating now was noodles and sandwiches due to the fact I could not cook food. When Saturday night came around this week, I once again hit my knees praying because I did not have enough gas money to get to church. After praying, God provided for me Sunday morning while walking to get in my truck. As I was walking to my truck, I found $10 on the sidewalk which was enough for me to get gas. I was not driving much during this time still. When I got to church someone brought me breakfast and took me out to lunch.

About the middle of August, I was praying for a place to stay and God provided a new place for me to stay with a family from Africa who housed people for free. The family was accustomed to having people live with them to help them out and then let them move forward in life without paying for food or rent. The family told me I could live with them until the beginning of the year. They invited me to their house one day and stated, "we were praying last night, and God told us to give you a place to stay". I never asked them for a place or told them I needed help. I simply went to God in prayer with it and He answered it through them. While I lived with them, they would not let me buy food. God provided all my food for me from August until December through this family.

I was still actively looking for jobs and going to interviews and I kept getting turned down. I realized God's hand was on the job opportunities keeping the door shut to it. Some of the jobs I was overqualified for like dish washing and still was told no. At this point in my journey of living on faith, I knew God's provision well enough that not getting the job did not bother me. God had provided for me for almost a year straight at this point and I knew He was going to be faithful to provide for me with or without a job. I started a new semester in college which kept me busy writing research papers. Not having a job actually proved to be more beneficial to me in the long run because of the heavy work load I encountered writing research papers. I literally did not have enough time to work a job. God shutting the door to the job opportunities was actually a blessing in disguise.

One-time close to the end of August I needed money for gas. I was going to chapel at a bible college and needed money to get to chapel on a Monday night. I never told anyone I was out of money. Every time I needed money for something I went to God with my need and thanked Him in advance for supplying my every need. He was already providing food and shelter for me for free which was a blessing. I went to an evangelism outreach on a Monday night. I was connected to an evangelism team that went out every Monday night. This night we went to an IKEA outlet to minister. After the ministry was over someone came and handed me a twenty-dollar bill saying

God bless you. I never told a single person I needed gas money to get to chapel. God used the person to provide for my need for gas. I was not driving much, and the gas money lasted to the end of August. As you can see God had fully provided for me for close to 9 months straight at this point living on faith in Him to provide.

September 2016

During the month of September, I spent a lot of time writing research papers. I was still actively applying for jobs only to be told no in personal or phone interviews. I realized God continued to keep the door shut on me working in the secular world. As Christians, we have to come to the realization that God is provider. God does and will use jobs to provide, but we have to remember God provided the job for us and He is providing through it. God can and will provide in other ways besides a job we just have to break our mindset from thinking like the world. God uses people to provide shelter, food, and money. The world wants us to think we have to go to college get a degree and work a full-time job being self-sufficient. God's way is to be fully dependent on Him which is completely opposite of the world. Romans 12:2 (NASB) states "Do not be conformed to the patterns of the world but be transformed by the renewing of your mind then you will know what the good, pleasing, and perfect will of God is". We have to renew our mind with the word of God, so we will know God's ways and not think like the world. The more you know God's ways the easier it gets to live and walk by faith. Romans 10:17 (NASB) "Faith comes by hearing and hearing by the word of God".

God provided in the month of September through a job again. Someone I knew sold cars at auctions and needed help transporting cars from South Carolina to North Carolina. During the month of September, I helped him out a couple of times which provided close to one hundred dollars for me during the month which was more than enough for me to live off of. I was not having to pay for rent or food. The only needs I was having to provide for was monthly car insurance and gas money. I never asked for the job. The guy who owned the business said God told him to get me to help him do it. The job was not a consistent job, but God provided my need for gas money with it during the month of September. September was a relatively quiet month other than doing evangelism outreaches and school work and it ended with me living another month completely on faith in God.

October 2016

October approached, and the weather changed as the winter season was beginning. I was still actively applying for jobs only to have God shut the door yet again. I was applying for anything and everything. I was not being picky. I was getting turned down for dish washing and serving jobs which I was well overqualified for. I realized God was keeping the door shut on the job opportunities. Let me remind you God had already provided rent and all my food for free during this time and I knew I was covered in that area. I was still in college full time which consumed most of my time. By the grace of God, I was able to keep a 4.0 GPA at this point in college. I was spending quite a bit of time writing research papers and studying though. All of my free time was devoted to either pursuing God or doing evangelism outreaches spreading the gospel. I made sure I kept obedient to what the Holy Spirit was leading me to do during this time. The weather was getting colder and I needed new winter clothes. I did not have the money to purchase winter clothes and I resorted to standing on scripture thanking God for His provision even though I could not see in it in the natural. I was walking by faith and not by sight. During this time, I was doing all night prayer meetings on Saturday nights which is when I thanked God for the new clothes I could not yet see.

God tells us we are not to worry about clothes that He will provide. Luke 12:27-28 (NASB) states "Consider the lilies, how they grow: they neither toil nor spin; but I tell you, not even Solomon in all his glory clothed himself like one of these. But if God so clothes the grass in the field, which is *alive* today and tomorrow is thrown into the furnace, how much more *will He clothe* you? You men of little faith!". During the winter season of my living on faith, I saw God provide clothing for me. At this point, I had not bought new clothes in a few years. I literally felt like I was living out the Israelites 40-year wilderness season as stated in Deuteronomy 29:5 (NASB) "I have led you forty years in the wilderness; your clothes have not worn out on you, and your sandal has not worn out on your foot." My clothes did not wear out did not fade much. Looking back, I see God's hand all over it, but it was time for new winter clothing. The area I lived in was high class and socially fit if you know what I mean. There were definite segregations between the upper and lower classes. After praying to God for new clothing, I was waiting for Him to provide. I was going through an extremely rough season and honestly, I think I had more unbelief than belief at this time.

A few days later after the Saturday all night prayer meeting a person came and handed me a brand-new American Eagle jacket and asked me to try it on to see if it fit. He responded you need some thermals to wear as well. A day or two later he brought me brand named sweaters and thermal shirts with the tags still on them. The individual price on each tag was well over $50 on each article of clothing. God answered the prayer for clothes within a few days of me asking Him which reminds me of the scripture 2 Timothy 2:13 (NASB) which states "If we are faithless, He remains faithful, for He cannot deny Himself". Even though I offered the prayer to God with more doubt than belief, God still proved Himself faithful. Along with the brand-new clothing, was enough money to provide for gas for a while which I did not pray for that Saturday night which shows you God provides for even when we do not ask Him for things as stated in Matthew 6:31-32 (NKJV) "Therefore do not worry, saying 'What shall we eat?' or 'What shall we drink?' or 'What shall we wear?' For after all these things the Gentiles seek. For your heavenly Father knows that you need all these things".

During October God provided through the car auction job as well. Between the answered prayer and helping a couple of times at the car auction God provided for all my needs. I was able to eat out occasionally and provide for all my gas money. I was not driving much during this time which helped. The distance from the house I was staying at to church was short. God fully provided another month for me. He provided new clothes through a person without me ever telling anyone I needed clothes. I simply prayed to God. God provided through the inconsistent jobs as well at the exact time when I needed the money for gas. I had survived another month living on nothing but faith in God and prayer.

November 2016

In November, I was still writing research papers and studying a lot. I was still actively applying for jobs and getting interviewed and still turned down. I was not being picky and was qualified to perform all the jobs I applied for. I saw it as God keeping the door shut to work. When you realize God's hand is on everything, you understand He controls the open and shut doors in your life. Isaiah 22:22 (NASB) states "Then I will set the key of the house of David on his shoulder, When He opens no one will shut, When He shuts no one will open". As I stated before, I used my free time to either spend time with God or evangelize. I related to an evangelism group from Africa which were basically like family. The evangelism outreach brought a new connection into my life for a short season which God used to provide for me through. I met a young lady and was led by the Holy Spirit to personally disciple her. I went to see her a couple times in November at her workplace. Each time before I went, I was about out of gas and I was out of money. The two times in November I went I did not eat before I went and could not afford food. Both times I went to see her at her workplace which had a food court I asked God to provide food for me. I never told her I needed food she just bought it both times. I realized it was God answering my prayer for food on both days it happened.

Two other times during the month of November I was out of money and gas with my back against the wall at my house. I was home alone and never told anyone I needed gas or money. I prayed and thanked God in advance for providing gas for me. I needed gas to get chapel and the library to do college work. While praying, I was thinking to myself I have no idea how I am going to make it. I have no gas, no money, and I am home alone. Both of these times I received a knock on the door randomly with a person handing me gas money not long after saying the prayer. I never told the person who brought the money I needed it. They had no reason to come by the house I was staying at. They simply told me "God told me to stop and give you this". God provided gas money straight to my front door two times this way. He sent a trustworthy messenger to hand me gas money at my front door.

Another time I was at home and needed gas money to go take a test for school. I was alone when I prayed. I never told anyone other than God I needed money. A couple hours later my roommate came home, and I received a phone call from her husband saying he was going to give me money for gas that I needed gas money. I never told anyone I needed gas money. 1knew it was God answering my prayer. Also, I was prompted by the Holy Spirit to go street witnessing with an evangelism team. I was out of gas and money with a job interview the next day in downtown Charlotte which was about 30 minutes away from where I lived. I had no idea how I was going to make it to the interview.

Isaiah 43:16-19 (NASB) states "Who makes a way through the sea And a path through the mighty waters, Who brings forth the chariot and the horse, The army and the mighty man (They will lie down together *and* not rise again; They have been quenched *and* extinguished like a wick): "Do not call to mind the former things, Or ponder things of the past. "Behold, I will do something new, now it will spring forth; Will you not be aware of it? I will even make a roadway in the wilderness, Rivers in the desert".

Similar to God parting the red sea and made a way of escape for Moses and the Israelites I knew God would make a way in my life for me to get to the job interview. He had already provided for me for a year solid at this point in my life on faith. I learned to quote and stand on the word of God. Instead of grumbling and complaining about life's issues I learned to quote and stand on the promises of God to provide. At the end of the street ministry, a person came and handed me gas money. They simply told me "God knows what you need". Once again God provided gas money exactly when I needed it.

Let me remind you that I am a giver. I am a firm believer in sowing and reaping as stated in Galatians. If you sow money you will reap money. When God tells me to give to others I give. It does not matter if it's the homeless alcoholic on the street or to a rich person at church. I simply follow the promptings of the Holy Spirit. Deuteronomy 15:10-11 (NASB) states "You shall generously give to him, and your heart shall not be grieved when you give to him, because for this thing the LORD your God will bless you in all your work and in all your undertakings. For the poor will never cease *to be* in the land; therefore, I command you, saying, 'You shall freely open your hand to your brother, to your needy and poor in your land." The key to giving is to give out of a loving pure heart. God is looking for a willing and obedient spirit and everything to be done with pure heart motives. James 3:13-18 (NASB) states "Who among you is wise and understanding? Let him show by his good behavior his deeds in the gentleness of wisdom. But if you have bitter jealousy and selfish ambition in your heart, do not be arrogant and *so* lie against the truth. This wisdom is not that which comes down from above, but is earthly, natural, demonic. For where jealousy and selfish ambition exist, there is disorder and every evil thing. But the wisdom from above is first pure, then peaceable, gentle, reasonable, full of mercy and good fruits, unwavering, without hypocrisy. And the seed whose fruit is righteousness is sown in peace by those who make peace."

Another form of provision during November came when God provided for me when I needed a computer. I had moved in with a new group of people and did not have a computer. I was going to college full time and stayed busy writing research papers, but I did not have my own computer. I never told anyone I needed a computer. I had already learned to go to God and not tell people what I needed at this point in the faith journey. I had literally seen God move so many times in my life I knew all I had to do was tell Him what I needed and expect for Him to provide for my need. Mark 11:24 (NASB) states ""Therefore I say to you, all things for which you pray and ask, believe that you have received them, and they will be granted you". One night after doing a street evangelism ministry God provided a computer for me. I never asked the person and the person gave me a desktop computer. He asked how I was doing in school and if I had a computer then said, "You are a lucky man God loves you I have a computer for you" after I replied "No".

To go along with the computer, God provided all the accessories I needed for it as well. The place I was staying had wireless internet and the computer did not come equipped with a wireless network card. I went to God in prayer knowing God would provide for me. After all He has just provided a computer for me so why would He not provide more. Psalm 37:4 (NASB) states "Delight yourself in the Lord and He will give you the desires of your heart". A few days later someone came up to me and told me "I was supposed to ask you how your computer is doing" because God told them to ask me how the computer was. God heard my prayer and relayed what He had heard to the gentleman. I told him it worked great besides needing a wireless internet card. The response I got was "Well you are not to worry about that God will provide your needs for you". About a week later I received a top brand wireless internet card along with food and gas money. God provided again, and I never asked God for the food or gas money. God simply provided for me because He knew I needed it and He loves me. After all, I am His son.

Also, during November God answered the prayer for me to see my son. It had been a long time since I had gotten to visit my son and I was really missing him. I did not have the money to drive to Tennessee and visit him. I was living by faith seeing God provide but the provision was only enough to get by and not with excess. I was not able to live freely during this journey of faith. I was praying to God on a nightly basis for my son telling God how much I missed him, and I really wanted to see him. One morning my roommate told me "Brother Mike God told me we are to drive to Tennessee to visit your family. Call your family and ask them when a good time is to visit them in the next couple of weeks and we will go visit them." God proved Himself faithful once again and answered my prayer of getting to visit my son. We went two weeks after my roommate approached me and they fully paid for everything including meals. God blessed me with a free trip all meals inclusive to visit my son and to witness to my family. All I did was tell God what I needed and waited on Him to provide it for me.

Finally, during this month, one Friday night I was led to take the girl I was discipling to a prophetic teaching. I did not have time to eat before we left, and I did not have money to buy food. I asked God to provide for me before we left to the prophetic meeting. After the prophetic meeting was over, the lady asked me if I was hungry, she would buy food because of the amazing encounter she had with God while at the prophetic meeting. She bought Taco Bell which at the time I was craving tacos. God provided the desire of my heart for me once again. November came to an end and I saw God move in powerful ways which built my faith. I realized I was seeing God move in ways most people will never get to experience in their lives.

December 2016

December came and with it came new challenges. The couple I was living with had people from Africa coming to live with them and I was going to have to find a new place to live. I did not have the money to get a place and inside I was cringing not exactly knowing what I was going to do. I was still applying for jobs and getting interviews only to be told no. I finally came to the conclusion God did not want me working and stopped applying for jobs by the end of December. God was providing for me it was just not through a job.

One time in December I was really craving pizza. I was eating lots of authentic African food because the people I lived with were from African and cooked authentic African food. The African family had no idea how to cook American food and were amazed at the American food I cooked while in their house. The ways we made scrambled eggs were completely different than each other. I was specifically craving pizza one day. I went to the pizza store and the cash register at the store was broke. I was talking to the manager about it and he told me to wait to see if they could get it working. The store was unable to ring up the pizzas which made them not able to sell because the cash register literally would not open. By this time, the store had no pizzas. They had gotten rid of all the pizzas because they could not take money due to the cash register being broke. While talking to the manager I started getting prophetic words for him. I was giving the words to the manager as God was giving them to me. The manager randomly asks what I wanted to eat, and I told him a large pepperoni pizza. He then made me a fresh pizza and handed it to me. He told me it was on the house that he appreciated me spreading the gospel, speaking into his life, and praying for him that there needed to be more people like me in the world. God gave me my heart's desire for a pizza, and He made a way where there was no way.

I told the testimony to a few people and one of them liked it so much they took me out to eat again telling me God provides. The gentlemen offered to take me out for whatever meal I chose to go to. The next meal I chose was a cheeseburger from Steak n Shake. He took me out to eat the following week which was another answered prayer and blessing. God showed up powerfully in my life twice giving me the desires of my heart. God delights in obedience and blesses it. Hosea 6:6 (NKJV) states "For I delight in loyalty rather than sacrifice, and in the knowledge of God rather than burnt offerings". 1 Samuel 15:22 (NKJV) states "Samuel said, "Has the LORD as much delight in burnt offerings and sacrifices as in obeying the voice of the LORD? Behold, to obey is better than sacrifice, *And* to heed than the fat of rams". God is looking for the willing and obedient to bless as stated in Isaiah 1:19 (NKJV) "If you are willing and obedient, you shall eat the good of the land". God is after our heart and wants us to be obedient. We are His children. We have to walk in obedience sacrificed fully to His will as He supplies all of our needs even our hearts desires when the time is right.

January 2017

January came and at this point I had lived off faith for over a year. I knew God as provider with enough testimonies I did not waiver much anymore as to having my needs met. With January coming, the need for a new place to stay arose. I moved out of the African residence a few days prior to January. Not long after I moved out, I received a call telling me to meet someone at church. They handed me large packs of drinks and food along with two hundred dollars cash. I was once again living in a place with no rent expense. The two hundred dollars was used to put gas in the truck and to help out other people. I went to the gas station to get gas and the person in the car behind me was highlighted in the spirit which meant God wanted to minster to them. God gave them a word about their family and finances and the lady was in tears crying. After giving the word, God told me to give the family fifty dollars which I did out of obedience. The law of sowing and reaping was playing out in my life as stated in Galatians 6:7 (NKJV) "Do not be deceived, God is not mocked; for whatever a man sows, that he will also reap". I received freely, and I also gave as led by the Holy Spirit.

During this time, God put it on a friend's heart to provide food a few days a week and a place to shower and rest. I took them up on it and ministered to them while there. I was living off mostly noodles, sandwiches, and pizzas at this time. After the two hundred dollars ran out, a person met with me the last two weeks in January taking me out to eat and handing me enough money for gas. God was providing all of my needs. With the extra money I had I was giving it away to homeless men and women as led by the Holy Spirit. Even though I did not have much, I was still freely giving as the Lord led.

Another time in January I was almost out of gas at a church service. I had some extra money set aside in my wallet to get gas after the service ended. At the end of the service the pastor took up an offering. The Holy Spirit prompted me to give all my money in the offering. Once again, I was thinking logically I have no idea how I am going to make it. I had close to a thirty-minute drive home and the gas light was on. I knew how far I could make it on the amount of gas left in my truck due to experience. Out of obedience and stepping out in faith I gave all the money I had in the offering. I got to the library to study and pray literally thinking I do not know how I am going to make it. I have no gas and I have no money. At this point, I only had enough gas to make it home and that was it. The Holy Spirit was prompting me to go to a conference this particular night which was close to a forty-five-minute drive away. I was thinking to myself I have no idea how this is going to work out. About ten minutes after being at the library praying, I received a text saying I had received money in the mail at a friend's house. The money was enough for me to fill my gas tank and eat on. As stated before, God knows what we need before we ask, and He has already seen our futures. We have to be obedient and take giant leaps of faith when we are prompted by the Holy Spirit. January came to a close and all my needs were met. I was spending a lot of time alone soaking in God's presence as He met all of my needs as stated in Psalm 23:1 (NKJV) "The Lord is my shepherd I shall not want".

February 2017

February came, and I was in full swing in school taking classes in two separate colleges. The free time I had was spent with God and doing school work. I was catching a lot of worship services and still going occasionally to get food and rest at the friend's house. I started working out consistently which provided a place to shower and get free Tootsie Rolls. During this walk on faith I learned how to embrace humble circumstances to a whole new level using 1 Thessalonians 5:16-18 (NKJV) which states "Rejoice always, pray without ceasing in everything give thanks for this is the will of God in Christ Jesus for you". I learned to enjoy the little things in life like watching a butterfly fly around on a sunny day. The little things a person can take for granted when caught up in the world.

A different type of receiving gas testimony occurred while I was in college in February. I attended a Monday night worship service because I really wanted to soak and rest in God's anointing. I encourage you to find a local prayer house and go to live sets to see how the spirit moves. It is amazing to see the worshippers sing exactly what you need to hear because they are led by God's spirit. When I arrived at the worship set, the gas light was on in the truck I drove. The next day I had chapel along with classes. While parking the truck, the gas light was on and the gas hand literally did not move any. The event occurred in the winter time with temperatures below freezing at night. When I got out of the truck I was thinking "I have no idea how I am going to make it". I have no money and my gas light is on with the gas hand on the gas gauge not moving any. I ended up staying at the prayer house this night to pray and rest all night in God's presence. I prayed for gas and thanked Him in advance for providing it. I got in the truck the following morning and started it. In my mind, I was expecting the gauge not to go up any. Remember the night before when I parked the gas light was on with the gas hand not moving any on the gas gauge. After I started the truck up, the gas hand went up to a quarter of tank with no gas light on. I thought maybe I am parked on a hill or there is an error and it will go down when I start to drive. The gas hand never went down, not instantly at least. God performed a miracle by supernaturally putting gas in the truck. To this day I have no idea how it happened other than God did a miracle by adding gas to my truck.

The last example I will use in this chapter is God's provision for a computer. I was in college during this time still and living solely on faith with no income. I had a desktop computer I used to do all my college work on. The computer had all my research papers and books on it along with other personal files. I had the desktop in my truck at the time because I was living between places. I was helping teach a two-day healing seminar on a weekend and a friend needed a ride to go eat lunch. I put the computer in a library to store it and it came up missing. I was taking online classes during this time and was about to start new classes and just bought new software. I had no idea how I was going to get a new computer. I went to God in prayer on a Saturday night with another heartfelt prayer telling God I needed a new computer for school. The prayer was more out of desperation, but it is ok because God honored it. The next day I got a text saying, "do not worry about your computer, I will take you to buy a new one". I never asked for a computer. A few days later, the person text me and told me to meet them at a store. While their they said "God told me to provide for all your needs, so I am here to provide for all your needs. Get all the food you need while we are here as well as the computer." The person bought me a brand-new laptop along with quite a few groceries and gave me close to $200.

A great part about this testimony about the laptop is while in the store I got to see God perform a miracle. After the merchandise was purchased, while walking to the door a lady was highlighted in the spirit. I know from experience to approach people when they are highlighted. When I got up to her, I saw the word anxiety wrote on her and asked if I could pray for her because she was full of anxiety. She let me pray. After the prayer, she asked me how I knew. The person I was with stated "he is a prophet and he is very good at what he does." She then started to test me about what I heard from God and asked me what else God was saying. The next thing God told me was about her personality. How she was open and not afraid to express her feelings to others. She was bold and spoke the truth and was not easily swayed by other opinions. The word was spot on, and then she immediately asked again what else God was showing me. The next thing God gave me was she was suffering from depression which was rooted in family issues. I told her what God told me and she opened up about a family member dying and the family members fighting over material things which was causing her to be depressed. She then confessed she had shoulder pain to the point she was restricted in arm movement and was scheduled to go for surgery. I asked to pray for her again. We prayed twice for her shoulder and God completely healed it. She said she felt it pop back into place and she could move it after the prayer. Even during providing for me, God had a blessing of love for someone else as well. God is good. February came to a close and all my needs were met building my faith and trust in God with the major provision I needed.

March 2017

March came, and I was still living rent free. God was still using people to provide me money when I needed it and I was faithful to give it out as led by the Holy Spirit. I saw God come through in food provision in a new way during this month. I saw God's hand on food provision for my life during this period when I was once again completely out of money. At this time, I was still in college and not working living on faith. I had about $13 in the bank and needed to wash clothes and buy toiletry items. I was literally out of food besides about 4 pieces of bread, 1 pack of ramen noodles, and crackers. I woke up the next morning knowing I needed money and prayed to God for food. The scripture Proverbs 10:3 came to my Spirit while praying which states "The LORD will not allow the righteous to hunger, But He will reject the craving of the wicked". I stood on this scripture after God dropped it in my spirit and rested knowing God was good for His word. I went to chapel and while there someone brought bread. At lunch time, someone came by and shared their lunch with me. A few hours later someone randomly offered their place in a food ministry which was enough food for a whole household for a week. God was faithful to His word and did not let me go hungry. Once again, He provided. I simply prayed, believed, and expected God to do what He said He would do.

A similar testimony occurred a couple of weeks later when I was prompted to go to a prayer meeting at a pre-church service. When I got to the service, I had no way to make it back to my house. My truck was literally out of gas with the gas light on. The previous night God had me give all my money away to a homeless person. I was prompted by the Holy Spirit to give them all the money I had, and I stepped out in faith. At this time, I had a deep personal revelation of God's provision in my life. The timing may not always be when I want it, but God has perfect timing. Out of obedience and love for God and His people I gave the homeless guy my money not knowing how I was going to make to church service and back home the next day. I drove to church service on faith and fumes. After the church service ended, a random person came up to me and handed me money. She simply said I was prompted by the Holy Spirit to give you this. I will do it the Pentecostal way in secret. March came to a close and once again all my needs were met by having faith in God.

April 2017

April brought new ways to see God's glory in provision. For the whole month, God provided food for me to eat while I did school work and ministry. A problem occurred though which was not too big for God. The truck I drove, which was a gift from God, needed breaks. The breaks were to the point of almost scraping metal. The high-pitched squeal was their cry for help informing me they needed to be replaced and quick. I did not have the money to get the breaks fixed so once again I went to my knees with the problem. I went to my knees and told God what I needed knowing God already knew what I needed before I asked him. It was not long after someone asked me how my truck was doing. I told them the truck is doing good, but the breaks needed fixed. I got a text message about a week later asking if I could meet a person at a certain time and place to get the truck breaks fixed. Along with having the breaks fixed at the mechanics house, the person gave me enough money to last for a while in cash. God put it on a person's heart to fix the truck breaks and give money to me. I once again thanked God for His working in my life. God is faithful even when we are unfaithful. The whole month God provided both gas and food to go along with the truck breaks. All my needs were met in April, and trust was being built stronger in God as He continued to meet my needs.

May 2017

May came with its own set of circumstances which God showed Himself faithful in. Matthew 6:33 (NKJV) states "Seek ye first His kingdom and righteousness and all these things will be added to you". I was seeking God's kingdom ministering as the Holy Spirit led. Along this time of living of faith, I really wanted a hot meal. God had provided food for me in numerous ways, but due to the living situations at the time most of the meals were not hot. I was living a life of sacrifice eating noodles and sandwiches mostly with pizza occasionally. One morning I was literally out of money to the point I could not wash clothes. Literally, all I had clean was a few items of clothing and the gas inside my truck with no extra money to even wash my dirty clothes. My heart's desire was to have a hot meal. I simply told God I really wanted a hot meal. Not long after saying the prayer, a person I was discipling called me for ministry. He was going through a rough season in life and needed counseling. After I got through ministering to him, he asked me if I wanted to go out to eat at a Chinese buffet and he gave me gas money for meeting him. God provided both food and money for me which was my heart's desire. God was faithful to His word once again and provided the desires of my heart for me.

A great thing about having the hot meal is not that God provided for me, rather it is that God used me to touch other people while eating at the restaurant. While eating at the Chinese buffet, God highlighted a construction worker who was eating with his coworkers. I approached him at the end of his meal because he was highlighted in the spirit and God gave me a heart of compassion for him. When he got up to leave the restaurant, I approached him, and God started speaking to my heart about Him. God told me he had a daughter he had a broken relationship with because he had made bad decisions in life and had driven his daughter away. His heart was burdened about restoration with his daughter. His daughter was not with him when God told me this and I stepped out in faith willing to be wrong if he did not have a daughter. The word was spot on for him. God even told me about insecurity issues he had which carried over into his leadership at his job site. God gave me a word of wisdom that the man's relationship with his daughter was going to be restored because God was moving behind the scenes. After talking to him, the restaurant hostess was highlighted. God told me to tell her not be so worried about her outward looks because it was inner beauty that mattered. The way she looked on the outside was consuming her. While delivering the word to her, God penetrated her heart and tears came to her eyes. God is good and is wanting to reach his people with love. In the middle of providing for me, God provided for two other people in the form of prophetic words spoken in due season as stated in Isaiah 50:4 (NKJV) "The Lord has given Me the tongue of the learned, that I should know how to speak a word in season to him who

I weary, He awakens me morning by morning, He awakens My ear to hear as the learned".

During this month, I was attending a conference and was invited to go to an outreach. The conference was a three-day conference which included outreaches on different days. I was going to go out to one of the outreaches, but the Holy Spirit kept prompting me to stay. While at the outreach, I was out of both gas and money and I never told a person. By now, I knew God's provision firsthand. A few hours after praying I got a text to meet a person at a restaurant, they wanted to buy me lunch. The lunch was provided for and they also got me gas which I never asked for either one. Later the same night, a person randomly came up to me and handed me a handful of money after they were prompted by God to give me the money. The Holy Spirit prompted me to give all of it away as an offering which I did. The next morning was Sunday and I attended church service as normal. When I got to service, a random person came and handed me an envelope saying, "God bless you thank you for praying for healing for me". I looked inside the envelope later and it was $500. After I got the money, I followed the Holy Spirit guidance because I knew God had plans for it. I obeyed God on giving it out to homeless people and missionaries as He prompted. Once again, God fully provided for all my needs without me telling anyone what I needed. I simply prayed to God telling Him what I needed knowing He would fully provide for all my needs. I gave most of the money away. One hundred dollars was given to a homeless person who broke down in tears crying because of the amount of money it was and he gave glory to God. The same homeless guy came up to me a few months later testifying about how God gave him his own place to stay after I prayed for him. A lady approached him and offered him a place to stay with full payment of utilities a few days after I was led to pray for him. He was speechless and utter amazement at how God provided for him giving all glory to God for the miracle in his life.

One last testimony during this month came when a friend asked me to disciple them on the prophetic. I was prompted by the Holy Spirit to meet them at a specific restaurant at a specific time. While at the restaurant, I was flowing in words of knowledge to a group of ladies who were eating at the restaurant. My friend told me "God told me to give you a $100" and handed me a $100. After I got the money, I knew God had plans for it and was obedient to do what God said with it which was give it away to homeless people. Also, God provided new tires for my truck. The tires on my truck started showing metal. I did not have the money to replace them, so I prayed. After praying, I thanked God in advance for the provision to come. Not long after praying I got a text to meet someone at a tire shop because God told them to buy me tires. Along with the tires, close to two hundred dollars was handed to me. God heard my prayer in secret and answered me in the open. May came to an end and all the needs were met once again by having faith in God.

June 2017

June arose along with new testimonies of God providing. An opportunity opened up for me to house and dog sit for a week which also provided food and money. All food was provided for housesitting and I even got offered BBQ meals which lasted for 3 days from a catering company thanks to a friend who blessed me as led by God. My car insurance came due and up to this point I had paid it thanks to money coming in provided fully by God. When it came due in June, the policy was changing because it was time to renew it and I did not have the money to pay for it. I gave to God and waited for Him to respond standing on the word in Matthew 6:33 (NASB) which states "Seek you first His Kingdom and righteousness and all these things will be added to you". A few days later someone offered to pay the car insurance for the month and said they would keep paying it until I could take over and I never asked for help. God provided once again answering my prayer.

One Saturday I was studying for a test after attending a morning prayer meeting and I started to leave to get food. I went to the truck and stopped. The Holy Spirit prompted me to stop and go back to the library. I went back to the library and not long after a friend of mine pulled up. He said he did not know why he came there but he took me out to eat. God's sovereignty was at work because I could not afford to buy food and the friend had no reason to come to library. He felt a prompting by the Holy Spirit and stepped out in it. Also, I was attending a prophetic class during the month of June at night. After class one night I was asked out to eat fully payed for by another person. Prior to this I had prayed because I had no money to buy food with. The person took me out to eat at Chick-Fil-A which was another answered prayer. A few days later I was at the prayer house praying and doing homework and what I thought was randomly going outside to take a break where I ran into a friend who was meeting his family for lunch. He had problems with his knees, and I prayed for his knees to be healed. The random stirring in my spirit to leave was God's sovereignty leading me to pray for the friend. After praying for him, I went back to doing homework. About an hour later he knocked on the door giving me a cupcake. God's sovereignty guides us more than we realize. Ruth encountered God's sovereignty as stated in Ruth 2:3 (NKJV) "Then she left and went and gleaned in the field after the reapers. And she happened to come to the part of the field belonging to Boaz, who was of the family Elimelech".

Other times in June I was completely out of food and gas and prayed to God and He provided money and gas exactly when I needed it. One time after getting money I was led to give some away at a gas station as led by the Holy Spirit and money to a friend at church as led. Jesus gave the charge in Matthew 10:7-8 (NKJV) which states "and as you go, preach, saying 'The Kingdom of Heaven is at hand.' Heal the sick, cleanse the lepers, raise the dead, cast out demons. Freely you have received, freely give". After all, "The earth is the Lord's, and all it contains, the world, and those who dwell in it" as stated in Psalm 24:1 (NASB). I am a firm believer in giving and will give the shirt off my back as led by the Holy Spirit. God provided all of June and another month passed as God met all my needs.

July 2017

July came around and once again God provided all of my needs. My car insurance was paid in full and offered to be paid in full until I graduated from college, so I could focus on my studies. My car tags came due and they were paid in full as well. Food and gas were completely provided for the whole month of July. God fully provide for all my needs as I was obedient to obey the promptings of the Holy Spirit. Numerous times God had me give money away to homeless people or pray for homeless people. God was providing in my life and using me as a vessel to spread His love to others.

I went to have my eyes checked in July because I needed contacts. I only had enough money to pay for my bill when I made the appointment. While at the doctor's office, God started speaking to me about the eye doctor and I was obedient to give the doctor the word. The doctor was in tears crying as God was ministering to her heart. After ministering to the doctor prophetically and getting my eyes checked, I was told my appointment was free along with full provision for contacts and glasses. God fully provided for the whole visit for me. All I had to do was step out in faith and minister prophetically as led by the Holy Spirit. Another month had gone by with full provision from God.

August thru October 2017

August, September, and October held more of the same occurrences of God providing in my life. No major provisions were made but all needs were met. At this point, I knew God could provide for all of my needs. The level of trust I had in provision came to a resting place in God. I knew God could provide for all my needs I just had to be obedient and step out as He led. I was once again in school and saw God fully provide for all of my food and finances. I learned to trust God in giving and with Him providing for all of my necessities. God fully provided for all of my needs and it had been close to two years at this point.

November 2017

November came again which marked two years of living on faith with no government help and no job. All food provision, gas money, toiletries, and rent were fully paid for by God. I had a lot of trust and faith in God at this point in my walk. Close to the end of November, I needed to find a new place to stay. The place I was staying abruptly ended and I was forced to find a new place. Two days were completely paid for me to stay in a hotel room followed by a room in a house offered by an individual. Also, during the month I needed to go meet family who was visiting me. When they came to visit, I had given all of my money away and needed gas. I had enough gas to get to where my family was, and I never told anyone I needed gas. When I met my family, who was in from out of state, a friend randomly came by and handed me money. I never told anyone I needed money. I simply prayed to God. I continued to give money away as led by God and by the end of the month I had close to $300 which was used to pay bills with. At this point, God had fully provided for me for two years. I knew God would provide all of my necessities by now. My faith and trust level for provision at this point was really high.

Beyond 2 years

Beyond two years, God still provided in the same way for another 10 months by having faith in Him. I would have random money deposited in the bank, another trip to Tennessee was fully provided for and once again I left Tennessee with more money than what I went with, another computer was bought for me after the laptop I had was broken, money was handed to me to pay for conferences and for teachings to attend as led by the Holy Spirit, numerous cell phones were provided, and I saw God supernaturally provide gas in my truck numerous times by praying while driving down the road and the gas hand moving up with the gas light on.

God has built my faith to a point that I know when a necessity is needed to be met all I have to do is go to God in prayer for it. During this time, I never completely ran out of food. I did not always eat what I wanted to eat, but God provided for me every step of the way. He proved Himself faithful to His word. I cannot say it was an easy process. My faith took time to develop to the level of having full expectancy in God. I did not just wake up one day and have full faith and expectancy in God.

There are also numerous times where God gave me the desires of my heart. Psalm 37:4 (NASB) states "Delight yourself in the LORD; And He will give you the desires of your heart". There was more than one time I was craving a certain type of food and God provided that type of food the exact day I was craving it. For example, one time I was really craving tacos but had no money to get them. I told God that morning I really wanted tacos. Around lunch time, a friend came by and asked me if I wanted tacos. Another time I was craving pizza and did the same thing. I simply spoke to God telling Him I really wanted pizza. Later in the day someone offered me pizza. Talking to God is like talking to people. All you have to do is tell Him your heart as stated in Psalm 62:8 (NASB) "Trust in Him at all times, O people; Pour out your heart before Him; God is a refuge for us". He already knows everything so really you are not telling Him anything He does not already know. Acts 1:24 (NASB) states "And they prayed and said, "You, Lord, who know the hearts of all men, show which one of these two You have chosen".

Seeing God, knowing His ways

For two years I lived on faith. I grew closer to God and grew a deeper understanding of His ways. Psalm 103:7 (NASB) states "He made known His ways to Moses, His acts to the sons of Israel." I have to admit it is much easier to live off faith when you have insight into God's ways. When you get a deep revelation of His provision and you know without a doubt that no matter what happens in life, He is going to provide for you your perspective of life changes completely. After all the bible says "Seek you first His kingdom and righteousness and all these things will be added unto you" in Matthew 6:33 (NASB). God is a good Father and is not going to let His children do without. You simply have to understand His ways.

Psalm 103:12 (NASB) states "Just as a father has compassion on *his* children, So the LORD has compassion on those who fear Him". God has compassion on the righteous. If God is calling you to step out in faith and give just trust God. He is the alpha and the omega. He has already seen the end. You simply have to trust God's leadership and the promptings of the Holy Spirit. If you know God is going to provide for you because it is a truth in the scripture and God is asking you to step out and give away all of your money, then I suggest you step out in faith and give all of your money as God leads. The reason being you reap what you sow, and God has already seen the end from the beginning. He knows what lies ahead in your life. God is not going to set you up for failure or leave you empty handed like a human would. God is asking you to step out because He already knows the end result of the giving. He knows what your tomorrow holds.

The more I live on faith the more excited I get about my journey with God. God is good in all His ways and once you have an expectancy that God will take care of you and provide it makes it easier to step out in faith. I have given and given by obeying the promptings of the Holy Spirit to see God provide in ways most people will never get to experience in their life. I have a deep understanding of God's ways to the point I know His provision and I can see Him in circumstances in my own life as well as other people's lives. I know God is not a liar and His word does not fall short. When God speaks or gives a promise or truth in the Bible His ways are to fulfill the truth or the promise. You can get to a place where you literally can see God in every detail of your life which is knowing His ways. You have a deep understanding of Him and be constantly aware of His hand and presence in your life on a daily basis.

You can see God in other people, situations, and circumstances and so forth. Seeing God in people manifests as love. It can be a hug from a person, a smile, a kind word, a pat on the back, or any other action that is uplifting and edifying. Seeing God in situations involves seeing His protection in your life. For instance, one time I was led to pray for protection then I got in the car and drove to a church life group meeting. While driving down the road I got to see God in the situation because He protected me from getting in a car wreck. I was on a two-lane road and I put on the turn signal to turn left and came to a stop. There was a car coming head on towards me in the other lane, so I could not turn. The car behind me was not paying attention and did not stop. He slammed his breaks the tires squealed and in order to avoid me he went to the left lane where the car was coming head on towards me. By the grace of God no one wrecked. The car behind me ended up stopped beside me. I literally looked beside my car and his car was at a complete stop beside me. Somehow the car coming head on did not hit him. I still have no idea how it all worked out. I know God was working behind the scenes and His hand was all in this situation protecting me from wrecking.

God is always moving behind the scenes. Jeremiah 29:11 (NASB) states "For I know the plans I have for you the plans to prosper you and not to harm you. The plans to give you a hope and a future." The revelation God gave me of this verse is God is working to make His plan work in our lives. He is constantly moving behind the scenes in ways we do not even know to bring His plan to fulfillment while we actively pursue the plan as well. I hope this has encouraged you and challenged you all to step into faith when God prompts you to. Just remember you reap what you sow and Luke 6:38 (NASB) "Give, and it will be given to you. They will pour into your lap a good measure—pressed down, shaken together, *and* running over. For by your standard of measure it will be measured to you in return." God is going to provide for you. You have to have the faith and trust in God to step out in faith when the Holy Spirit prompts you to.

Happy giving guys.
God bless you and Jesus loves you.

References

[1]Expectancy. (1995). In *Strong's exhaustive concordance: New American standard Bible*. (Updated ed.). Retrieved from http://www.biblestudytools.com/concordances/strongs-exhaustive-concordance

[2]Rhema. (1995). In *Strong's exhaustive concordance: New American standard Bible*. (Updated ed.). Retrieved from http://www.biblestudytools.com/concordances/strongs-exhaustive-concordance

[3]Logos. (1995). In *Strong's exhaustive concordance: New American standard Bible*. (Updated ed.). Retrieved from http://www.biblestudytools.com/concordances/strongs-exhaustive-concordance

Donations

This book was written out of obedience to God. God told me to write this book to help out others. If you felt led, you can donate to Mike Mayfield Ministries at

http://www.mikemayfileministries.com.

The book is a free publication intended to help others look to Jesus for freedom. God bless you all!!!

Thank you all for reading and for your support.

Jesus

Loves

You